Laurie Cabot's Book of Visions

by Laurie Cabot

with

Penny Cabot &

Christopher Penczak

I0112294

**COPPER
CAULDRON**
PUBLISHING

Credits

Writing: Laurie Cabot, Penny Cabot, Christopher Penczak
Cover: Rory McCracken
Editing: Tina Whittle
Copy Editing: Kathy Pezok, Leeon Pezok
Layout & Publishing: Steve Kenson

For more information visit:
lauriecabot.com
christopherpenczak.com
coppercauldronpublishing.com

ISBN 978-1-940755-11-3, First Printing, Printed in the U.S.A.

Disclaimer

This book of visions and meditations, with all exercises, spells, rituals, formulas, and advice in it are not substitutes for professional medical advice. Please confer with a medical professional before using any herbs, remedies, or teas in any manner. Unless specifically indicated, formulas are not intended to be consumed or ingested. Author and publisher assume no responsibility for those using this material in an inappropriate manner.

Table of Contents

INTRODUCTION 1
CHAPTER 1: MEDITATION...7
  Preparation for the Work 10
CHAPTER 2: FOUNDATIONAL MEDITATIONS.............................17
  The Apple Meditation 17
  Polarization Meditation 20
  Polarized Breathing 21
  Positive Breathing 21
  Negative Breathing 22
  Druid Candle Meditation 23
  The Crystal Door Mind Travel Meditation..................................23
  Out of Body Voyage 26
CHAPTER 3: PROTECTION MAJICK..29
  Protection Shield Meditation 30
  White Light Pentacles 33
    Fig. 1: Pentacle...33
  The Rosicrucian Protection Arrow 34
    Fig. 2: Rosicrucian Double Arrow 35
  White Light Dragons..35
  Golden Ring and Star of Protection 37
CHAPTER 4: ENERGY WORK & HEALING MEDITATIONS.........39
  The Pink Star Journey 40
  The Three Cauldrons..43
  The Egyptian Sun 45
  Healing the World 47
CHAPTER 5: MEDITATIONS FOR LIFE 49
  The Majick Mirror 49
  Prosperity Meditation 51
  Love Meditation 53
  Inner Child Healing Meditation 54
  The Forest of Mystery 56
CHAPTER 6: ANIMAL SPIRITS 59
  The Cat 60
  The Flight of the Owl 62
  White Rabbit...64
  The Journey of the Horse..66
  The Healing Bees...69

The Changing Snake 73
The Crow of Protection 76
The Realm of the Lion 78
Groundhog 80
The Darkness of the Mole 83
Swimming with the Dolphin..87
The Dreaming Bear...89
The God of the Deer Tribe 92

CHAPTER 7: THE PATH OF THE WITCH **97**
The Majick Room..97
The Witch's Walk 104
Liquid Moonlight..106
Balance of the Moon and Sun 107
The Vision of the Wishing Candle 109
The Ancestors..110
The Mysterious Planet Vulcan 112
The Twin of Sparta 114
Root Race Meditation 116
The Crystal Wheel Meditation 121
The Weaver of the Midnight Sky 124

CHAPTER 8: THE ELEMENTAL POWERS **127**
Penny's Green Balance Meditation 127
The Element of Earth 129
The Element of Air 131
The Element of Fire 132
The Element of Water 135
Fig. 3: Elemental Triangles...*138*
The Faery Realm..138
Rowan Tree Meditation..141
Lord of the Forest..143
Fig. 4: The Green Man *143*
Earth Healing Meditation 145
Healing Water..148
Ocean Meditation..151

CHAPTER 9: EGYPTIAN VISIONS..**153**
Thoth-Hermes and the Emerald Tablet.......................................154
The Temple of Isis..157
The Tomb of Osiris 158
Flying with Horus 162
Fig. 5: Horus as the Hawk...*163*
The Barge of Ra 165

Fig. 6: The Eye of Ra *166*
The Home of Hathor 169
The Meditation of Sekhmet 171
The Temple of Cats 173
The Pyramid and the Sphinx 176
CHAPTER 10: JOURNEYS IN AVALON **181**
The Land of Camelot...181
The Arthurian Knight 183
Fig. 7: The Round Table..*184*
The Sword of King Arthur...186
The Heart of Queen Guinevere..190
The Path of Merlin 192
Fig. 8: Three Ring Knot *194*
Fig. 9: The Flag of Wales...*196*
Avalon and the Ladies of the Lake 198
The Pendragon 202
CHAPTER 11: WALKING WITH THE CELTIC GODS..................**205**
Three Spirals of the Goddesses 205
Fig. 10: Triple Spiral *206*
The Sun God Lugh 208
The Awen of Taliesin the Bard 210
Fig. 11: Awen...*212*
The Cauldron of Cerridwen...213
The Vision of Branwen: Hold Your Brothers Close.........................217
Mother Modron Home Blessings 220
The Witch's Eyes with the Morrigan 223
The Goddess of Justice Macha 224
The Goddess Arianrhod 225
Visiting Dagda, the Good God...229
The Nine Children of Danu 232
ABOUT THE AUTHOR..**239**

Introduction

What is the purpose of meditation in Witchcraft? How has it come to be in Witchcraft culture and in our methods? Many people believe only the stereotypes of Witches, erroneously assuming that Witchcraft has nothing to do with spirituality and meditation, but meditation is a tool of the Witch as much as any candle or broom. Meditation is using our alpha level, our psychic level of awareness, to get in touch with the otherworld, and with the gods and goddesses of the otherworld. Meditation enhances our majick, making it more powerful for the good of all. In modern times, meditation can put you in touch with nature and the gods no matter where you live. You can live in New York City, in a high-rise building, and still reach those levels of understanding as you use meditation to meld yourself into nature and the conscious energy of nature.

Meditation helps us remember that everything is natural and part of the living field of energy. Sidewalks are made of natural things. Bricks and concrete are natural. Petroleum is not foreign to the Earth, even though it is worked by humans and can be harder to get in touch with spiritually. In a city setting, getting in touch with the pulse of nature is not as easy as it is in the country or a small town. Meditation helps us slow down and experience what is around us, particularly in our fast-paced lives. Even when we live in a more natural setting, most of us, as modern humans, have lost a great deal of our ability to connect with it. Meditation upon nature can help reset our relationship with the natural world.

Many people feel that meditation is a mysterious thing, but it is simply closing your eyes for more than three minutes, putting you into an alpha state of brainwaves. This state helps you access your psychic senses and better perceive the otherworld. Through meditation, you develop a different understanding of the animals, plants, minerals, planets, and the gods and goddesses themselves. Your understanding of the world you already live in, with its many invisible forces already around you, grows deeper with each practice, and you grow as a Witch.

Once you have meditated with one animal, even if you knew nothing about it before you began, you can understand the nature of that animal. You will be as knowledgeable as anyone who has studied it, but your knowledge will be through your direct experience of its energy and presence. Meditation will put you in touch with what is real.

Meditation is like controlled sleep, a form of conscious sleeping. If you don't sleep well at night, meditation during the day can help catch you up and restore your vital energy. Every fifteen minutes in alpha brainwaves is like three hours of sleep in terms of rejuvenating the body. Many people working in fields that require long shifts, like doctors, will meditate or simply close their eyes for fifteen minutes and then wake up refreshed. They are using their alpha level, not deep sleep, to catch up on their rest.

Everyone already does meditation to some extent. Simply by closing your eyes, your brain drops into alpha. You do it when you sleep at night. Some people have such high expectations of what meditation is, expecting it to be bombastic, with bells and whistles and explosions of all sorts to tell them they are in meditation. That is not the way it happens. And it shouldn't be, for meditation is natural. You don't have to ride a rollercoaster to get into the state of meditation. It's a normal sensation, and you might not even realize you are there. People who have difficulties expect more, thinking they are missing something, but they are not actually missing anything. They are not allowing themselves to experience what is already naturally happening.

Eastern traditions appear to use meditation for simple relaxation, and while that can be a by-product, that is not what we as Witches are about in our meditative practices. Our meditations—and often our psychic visions and journey experiences—are often difficult for us, because our practice is about enhancing our work as Witches, which can be as confrontational as it is healing. We encounter beings from the otherworld and use meditative practices as a part of our majick, to project for the outcome of what we wish to have happen in our lives. Meditation techniques become part of what we use to cast our spells.

The first "meditations" I learned from my own mother were prayers. Mother taught me the "Now I lay me down to sleep" prayer before bed. While done in a Christian context, the repetition of words and intentions was quite meditative. Later in my teens, I first heard about meditation and realized how it was similar to much of the psychic work my Witchcraft teacher Felicity had taught me. I realized I was already doing forms of meditation, drifting into alpha and receiving creative ideas and mystical contact. Even today, some of my strongest meditation experiences happen at night, right before sleep.

Felicity simply called it majick or power, but she would have us close our eyes and enter into a vision. We would envision what we wished to create in our minds, seeing and sensing what was going to happen. Her favorite was conjuring up the wind to blow feathers away, to prove you could call the wind. She would suggest we would "see"—or really *feel*—the wind, as we saw clouds moving and billowing. And she taught that you did not always have to close your eyes to see things happening. She was teaching a form of meditation and thought projection at the same time, the foundation of so much popular lore on visualization and positive thinking that would come later in the greater culture.

While most meditation is with your eyes closed, sometimes you meditate with your eyes open. When you soft focus your eyes and stare out a window, you are meditating because your brain goes into alpha level. Listening to music helps you visualize and paint a picture by the music, allowing you to enter into meditation. Symphonic or even popular music can "suggest" certain scenes, such as wooded areas with dancing fairies. Symphony titles from classical music suggest images from the composer. This kind of induced imagery from music is a form of meditation as well. Felicity would also teach us to gaze into bowls of water mixed with black ink, like a dark mirror. As you entered into a meditative state by simply focusing upon the black water, you would begin to perceive imagery, pictures, and messages rising up in your mind, even with your eyes open. It's the same principle that we often use today with Tarot, allowing images and messages to rise up from the pictures as we gaze upon the cards.

Later my friend Master Thomas of the Rosicrucians would teach contemplative exercises. He never called them meditations, but he gave you images to focus on, to bring to life, that reflected the teaching he was giving. He would often have us imagine the pebble thrown into the still pond. We would gaze at the image of the waves rippling from where the pebble entered outward to the shore and then the waves returning to where they began, and the patterns created by the waves. These images were the basis for understanding that every action has its reaction and consequence. Everything is influencing everything else. This is still an idea I teach my students through the Hermetic Principles of *The Kybalion*.

While many traditions will focus on a more passive technique to empty the mind and still the thoughts, we all can't sit on a mountain and hum for twenty years. The basis of Witchcraft meditation is to use specific techniques to enter into an altered state, using our science of the craft. Through this, we learn how to influence and control light energy in our brain and body. We learn how to send and absorb light. For me, this is the most fundamental thing in Witchcraft. With it, you can accomplish anything else in the Craft. Developing our meditative skills is like developing a muscle that will be the basis for all else to come. Once we get counted down into an alpha state, we use our light energy to connect, communicate, and experience the subtle world of nature and the otherworldly reality of the gods. Though many other religious traditions, both east and west, do similar communication with gods and spirits, it's not emphasized as a part of meditation, yet this is a crucial skill for the Witch.

One of my most powerful contacts with deity early in my adult life was with the goddess Isis. When I first saw her on the screen of my mind, she was like a pinprick in the distance. As I kept talking to her in my mind, she kept moving towards me, getting larger and larger. By the time she reached me, she was gigantic in proportion. My body was the size of her big toe, and she passed right through me. It was frightening and truly awesome. Through this image, she was letting me know the vast power she is, her own status and magnificence. I was astounded. Even though I made contact, and on some level still thought I was in control, I was not. I had no control once I made contact. She was the one who was in control. It took my breath away, mixing elation and fear, as I had never quite had something like that happen in a meditation before. I had never felt out of control before. One of the first things I still teach is how to form a protection shield, and how to remain in control when things form on the screen of your mind, protecting yourself on the mental, physical and spiritual levels. The gods, however, are more powerful than we are, and while their intention isn't to harm us, they do show us that we are not always in control. Isis is a magician from the otherworld, and she showed me that she was. From that point I learned the reality of the otherworld and the ancient ones, as they have been living there for centuries, perfecting their majick.

Isis taught me to be more respectful when calling upon her, and all the gods. She also respected me by showing me that she was real, giving me a precise formula for a potion with "real" historic ingredients my mind had no conscious knowledge of. That oil is still used today to help connect with her. She has since helped me many times in my life.

The gods have taught me how they can, in some places, not only communicate through the veil between worlds, but break through the veil and come to us. We don't break through the veil to come to them. They come to us, or sometimes, we create together an in-between meeting place we can visualize. Sometimes we are allowed to see the otherworld, or are even invited for a short time into it, but we cannot live in their world. We can invite them into our lives. Our prayers, rituals, and meditations are a signal for them to come to us, but they don't have to do so. The gods don't answer everyone. Each deity is unique with unique relationships.

As Witches, we ask for their help in our majick when necessary. We honor the ancient ones, but we don't grovel or supplicate. We honor the gods. We don't really worship them in the way that people use the word "worship." We venerate them. Groveling is not the way of the Witch. We don't get down upon our knees and beat our chests.

Sadly for us, many of the terms we use today in English are adaptions from the Burning Times. Christianity has named, renamed, and co-opted our understanding and expectations of spiritual and religious experiences. Their ways are not the ways of the Witch, and modern Witches are still working to untangle our words and terms from that Christian understanding. The addition of science to ancient Hermetic philosophy is certainly helping us understand our differences. As we continue to meditate directly with the gods, spirits, and nature, our experiences will directly inform us in reclaiming the old ways and pioneering the new ways. They will add to our vision of the Craft and the evolution of our community and traditions.

Chapter 1: Meditation

Meditation is the master key to majick, psychic development, and spiritual evolution. A lot of people are confused about what meditation is, thinking it requires an absence of thoughts, but meditation is really just focused attention. It is a technique to shift our brainwaves, and when our brainwaves enter different states, we gain different abilities and perceptions.

My life's work has been teaching the science of Witchcraft to the world at large, and the understanding of the brainwave state of alpha is at the heart of my teachings. Our brainwaves can be measured in cycles per second, also known as hertz (Hz), and categorized into four main brainwave states. Our waking consciousness is at beta level, in the 14-24 Hz range. This is our state of active awareness. We are alert, awake, and emphasize logic, reason, and linear understanding. Below beta is alpha level, at 7-14 Hz. Alpha occurs when we are resting, but this daydream state is where intuition, non-linear thinking, creativity, and psychic perceptions are active. Below alpha is theta, ranging from 3-7 Hz. While alpha allows us to easily interact with the waking world, in theta, we are withdrawing from the world, still retaining control over bodily functions even as we experience clearer inner visions. Lastly there is the delta state at 0-3 Hz, the deepest trance where there is no real linear thought and we are able to experience astral travel and out-of-body states.

Alpha allows us to not only receive information, but also to direct energy, for information is simply a form of energy. We can direct energy to heal, to manifest, and to make contact between the worlds to communicate with all manner of spirits and beings. Attaining alpha state is not as hard as many people think. It's quite natural, so natural that you don't always consciously realize you are in alpha. Don't think that to be successful you have to be oblivious to the outside world. At times you will slip down into theta, but for most of the time, you'll be aware of your environment. You will not become catatonic when successfully working in alpha. Like any skill, practice is the key. Practice it daily, even if only for five or ten minutes. Much like physical exercise, repetition is needed to learn it and to benefit from it.

We naturally experience all of these states during the course of our sleeping and dreaming, but meditation techniques allow us to consciously control the shift in our brainwave states in and out of the waking beta state, yet still interact, engage, and remember our experiences in the deeper levels. If you close your eyes for three minutes, your body automatically goes into alpha state. Different meditation techniques work differently for people, and various spiritual traditions will emphasize one technique over another. Some practitioners focus on the breath; others use special words called mantras to be repeated silently. Many focus their gaze upon an object, picture, or mandala. Some chant. In the Cabot Tradition of Witchcraft, we use a technique called the Crystal Countdown.

The Crystal Countdown uses visualized numbers and colors to help us achieve alpha state, programming us through a sequence of intended visualizations to lower our brainwaves and open us to non-linear information and energy. We draw from universal ideas of number and color in our understanding of alpha and use of the Crystal Countdown. I look to the Greek philosopher Pythagoras as the foundation of this system. Many believe he was trained by the Celts and that this knowledge is a part of our Celtic heritage, though there is no hard evidence of this. In the present time, Celtic Witches still use color, number, and scientific understanding of brain states to commune with their gods and work their majick.

The physical relaxation that comes with meditation lowers the blood pressure and stimulates the release of balancing hormones and chemicals. While meditation can be a part of anyone's life, since science is beginning to recognize that a meditation practice improves overall health and well-being, those of us who follow a majickal spiritual path believe that meditation opens the door to inner vision and psychic travel. Our mind's eye becomes a screen and portal, bringing things to us or to sending them outward into the spiritual worlds. While they are often unfamiliar to us today, these worlds were well charted by our ancestors and recorded in our myths and stories. There we can interact with spirits, powers, and deities; each can hold wisdom, healing, and power. Interacting with these beings and landscapes can transform us on the path of the Witch.

While we often describe these experiences as visionary, with most people describing them through the sense of sight, not everyone has a clear inner vision. Some people work through all the psychic senses. You'll find alpha visions to be much like your dreams, so however you normally dream will be the way you'll experience these guided meditations. Some people get a strong sense of feeling, or simply knowing what is happening, without a clear inner vision. Many hear the voices of the gods and spirits clearly. Others struggle, but with practice, they begin to interact with the gods and spirits and know they are there, even if they are not easily perceived. The faculty that allows us to interact with these beings is akin to imagination, for imagination is one of our most majickal gifts. Sometimes you might feel like you are "making it up" with your imagination, but you are simply giving the spirits and gods a vessel in your mind's eye through which they can interact. While our understanding of these teachings is grounded in modern Witchcraft and majick, you can see a similar and long-standing tradition in the East with the esoteric Buddhists and Hindus.

The information you receive in alpha will be interpreted in images and ideas you already know. They are familiar because they are already programmed in our consciousness and are easy to access, but we must nonetheless learn to interpret them. Spirits will communicate with you by showing you an image in your brain. They are looking for common language and understanding. Since our modern minds are programmed differently from our ancestors—without the same mythic stories, no longer living in the landscape of our gods—we need to reach out and learn more, to expand the vocabulary of our language between us and them. Learning mythology, the stories of the goddesses and gods, helps provide an interface of symbols, images, and language for us to use when we interact with them.

PREPARATION FOR THE WORK

The guided meditations, or majickal visions, of this book are combinations of meditations and rituals used to evoke the attention and favor of various spirits, heroes, and deities from our modern traditions of Witchcraft. They reach back into history to commune with ancient entities whom Witches seek for aid and understanding. It can help if you prepare for the work rather than enter it haphazardly.

Many of the visions will suggest lighting a special candle or incense and then reciting a particular verse to evoke the attention of the spirit we seek. It's like sending a message ahead before you knock on someone's door, letting them know you wish to come. All of these entities have their own will and desires, and sometimes their response will be "no" and nothing will happen in the vision, or you'll enter into alpha and go somewhere, but the expected spirit will be nowhere to be found. While frustrating, this is normal, and is actually a good sign you are going beyond your personal imagination to real contact. You aren't home for everyone who wants to knock on your door, are you? It's the same for the gods and spirits.

So my first suggestion is to read through the entire vision first, determining what you will need, if anything, and familiarizing yourself with the sequence of events. Many people will record the meditation slowly and thoughtfully in their own voice and place some relaxing meditation music on to drown out the outside sounds of neighbors or family and help keep focus. Recording yourself is an excellent way to induce trance once you get used to the sound of your recorded voice.

Make your space comfortable. Set up your altar and any items like candles, incense, oils, or other objects. Lower the lighting. Light your candles. Clear quartz, as a point or a sphere, can be an excellent tool to help you stay clear and attentive. You can have one before you or a small one in your hands, cleansed and charged for psychic clarity and focus. If you are unfamiliar with working with tools, including cleansing them and charging them, simple instructions can be found in *Power of the Witch, Laurie Cabot's Book of Spells and Enchantments,* or *Laurie Cabot's Book of Shadows.*

Some people like to lie down for meditation. For some deep meditations that can be advised, but if you are prone to falling asleep, I would suggest sitting up in a straight back chair, feet flat on the floor, and hands in your lap. Make sure you have everything with you that you will need, so nothing will distract you when it's time to begin.

The Crystal Countdown

The Crystal Countdown is the primary technique I teach and use in my Witchcraft classes. It is like the bookends to a meditation. One can start a vision with the countdown, and end with the count-up. The work between the countdown and count-up will be different every time. Once you are well-versed in meditation, you might find yourself spontaneously going into visions and returning, using the imagery and sensation from the intended destination. That is perfectly fine, but if you ever have difficulty, return to the structure of the Crystal Countdown to achieve alpha level and to return to beta.

The Crystal Countdown uses the image of a crystal-clear rainbow of light, partnered with numbers, to lower your brainwaves to alpha. The colored light holds information and energy. Visualizing colored light with our eyes closed helps activate our pineal gland and have psychic information penetrate our consciousness. This pineal gland is your third eye, often called your mind's eye, and it receives and directs psychic energy. The mind's eye can be a gateway for projecting our awareness to different levels of consciousness to meet different entities and spirits. Some would say you are going to the spirit. Others say you bring the spirit world to you through the screen of the mind. In either case, the effect and experience are the same, so we focus on getting helpful and accurate information and energy when working with the spirits.

You will perceive your mind's eye, or the screen of your mind, in front of you, at the brow, though some project their awareness in the space before their face. Remember that our "vision" and "seeing" is an inward seeing, and not with the physical eyes. It is really a perception that is beyond physical vision, but which can be described using the same terms and words we use for physical vision.

The more you relax into alpha, the easier it will be. "Trying too hard" can keep us in beta level. Done successfully, it's like having a fun daydream or purposely letting your mind wander. Remember it's supposed to be relaxing overall, so if you are not relaxing, take a break and try again later.

Prepare your space and yourself. Get into a comfortable position and close your eyes. Breathe deep and relax. Relax all the muscles around your eyes and eyelids. Relax your jaw. Feel the warmth on the top of your head and feel warmth over your forehead down your face and shoulders, down your spine, over your arms and fingertips. Feel the warmth down your thighs and your shins, over and under your feet. Relax. Look at the screen of your mind's eye; keep your eyes closed and relax. You are using your brain and not the muscles in your eyes. Look at the screen of your mind.

See the number seven, and see the color red.

See the number six, and see the color orange.

See the number five, and see the color yellow.

See the number four, and see the color green.

See the number three, and see the color blue.

See the number two, and see the color indigo; see the midnight sky.

See the number one, and see the color orchid.

You are now in alpha level. Continue to slowly count from ten to one, at which time you will be in a more perfect level.

Ten, nine, eight, seven, six, five, four, three, two, one.

You are now at your innermost level where everything you do will be accurate and correct, and this is so.

Perform any meditative vision or psychic work you want to do.

When you are done, return yourself back up to beta level by counting up. To count up, first erase the screen of your mind with your hand, dismissing it.

Give yourself Total Health Clearance by placing your hand above your head, and with a sweeping motion, bringing it down in front of your body. At your solar plexus, push your hand out and away from the body.

Count from one to ten without colors. Count from one to seven without colors. Open your eyes.

I recommend memorizing these steps, starting with the color and number combinations. The number and color combinations can manifest in any way that works well for you. You can see a red seven on a white, black, or clear screen. You can see a large black number seven on a red background. You can even envision drawing or writing the letters upon the screen with your hand. The number can be "hollow," an outline filled with the appropriate color, or a black or white number that changes to the appropriate color. Any and all of these techniques work. The intention of the number and the corresponding color, in any manifestation, is key.

If you have difficulty with the colors, try to remember things associated with the color, and conjure the memory of that item. Evoking powerful memories and images helps greatly. Draw from your memory. For example, imagine a delicious red apple or stop sign for red. A pumpkin, carrot, or orange juice can be used for orange. A banana, lemon, or canary can be used for yellow. Vibrant grass, a leaf, a green traffic light, or an emerald jewel can be used for green. The clear sky, a clear lake, or the tropical ocean works for blue. Indigo is the color of the clear midnight sky, or an eggplant. Orchid is the color of the flower, though a light lilac or pale lavender flower would work too.

This simple meditation is the building block for all others. It is as easy as getting to number one and orchid. At that point, you are successfully in alpha, even if you don't think you are. The shift in color and number will adjust the flow of your energy and brainwaves. While either is effective, the combination of the two makes this a powerful and foolproof technique. This second countdown just gets you deeper and more relaxed.

The instructions of the subsequent meditations will not include the Crystal Countdown. Use this method as it is effective and powerful, particularly if you are just starting out. But if you have other methods of getting into a meditative state, or naturally can shift your awareness into meditative vision, use what works best for you.

Chapter 2: Foundational Meditations

Just like learning any new skill, there are basic foundational exercises you should practice to build your abilities and understanding. Just like a musician must learn scales or a painter must learn to blend colors, a Witch must learn how to enter into and out of alpha, and how to direct energy and receive energy as information. Just because something is simple and foundational doesn't mean it isn't as important as bigger acts of majick. There are several powerful techniques I teach to my first-degree students to help build their psychic ability, but they are exercises we continue to do even as we progress in our Witchcraft. Use these foundational meditations to help build your skills, but come back to them time and again to strengthen yourself.

THE APPLE MEDITATION

The first meditation I teach after the Crystal Countdown is the Apple Meditation. Showing up in our mythologies and images of the Witch, the apple is a sacred Witch symbol. Associated with the otherworld realm of Avalon—also known as Apple Isle or the Land of the Witches—we see it as a symbol of wisdom and protection. If you cut an apple in half crossways, you'll find the image of the five-pointed pentagram made from the seeds. The tree itself is associated with faeries, majick, and healing.

The apple meditation teaches us how to connect to the screen of the mind and use it to draw something specific we desire. In this case, we practice with an apple. Through your intention, you are drawing to yourself the energy and aura of a real apple existing somewhere in the world. It might exist in your neighbor's kitchen, hanging on a tree, or sitting on the shelf of some grocery store many miles away from you, but you are connecting to a real apple. This skill helps us when we want to connect to different people and places through the screen of the mind.

Enter into alpha using the Crystal Countdown. Call upon the screen of your mind. With your intention, draw to your screen the image, energy, and aura of an apple. Visualize the shape of the apple, and let the details come through. Each time it will be a different apple, so each time, the details will be different. Sense the apple vividly upon the screen of your mind, as if it would be in front of you physically.

With each moment, the details become clearer as the image comes in focus. With your eyes still closed, physically reach up onto the screen of your mind and touch the apple. Feel its skin. Grasp the apple with your forefinger, middle finger, and thumb. These are three acupressure points that will activate your psychic senses more deeply. They are points where we take in more information. The index finger helps us perceive, and the middle finger helps us remember, so using both at once helps firmly plant the experience in your memory.

Cup the apple in your hand. Sense the texture, feeling the smooth skin. Look closely at it. Notice all the details, all the ridges and bumps. Notice the color of the apple, as not all apples are red. Smell the aroma of the apple. You can open the apple up, look inside at the star of seeds. As you do, you might even find yourself automatically tasting the apple, determining its ripeness. Anything you do to the apple on the screen of your mind can be easily reversed, restoring the apple to the shape it was when you first saw it.

When you are done, place the apple back upon the screen of your mind. Restore the image to its original state. Erase the apple from the screen using your hand, as if you are erasing a blackboard or wipe board. Erasing the image releases the aura of the apple, and integrating your hand motions with this action while you are in an alpha state will help you with future readings and ritual work. Give yourself Total Health Clearance and count yourself back up to beta.

The Apple Meditation is a safe and easy way for us to practice, and the image and energy of the apple connects us to our Witchcraft ancestors and the wisdom and spirit of the apple and Avalon. All of your sensory experiences create the way your psychic mind processes the information. The energy of the apple will enter your screen, but it is also interacting with your own aura and energy body once it is upon the screen. You'll see it through your third eye, the screen of your mind. You can also feel it in the solar plexus as a "gut feeling."

Don't be discouraged if your apple doesn't quite look real. Sometimes it can look like a picture, sketch, or cartoon of an apple. Sometimes the image is "real," but cloudy and less distinct. These are all ways that our mind processes the information, but it is still real. The more you practice, the easier it will become, and the more you will understand how you receive and perceive psychic information. Tuning into your senses and using your physical gestures can greatly improve the experience. Take a deep breath to smell. Lick your lips to taste. Pause and listen. All of these senses will provide psychic information to you if you become aware. As with all meditation and psychic information, relax and let it come. Don't try to force it to conform to how you believe it should look or be.

POLARIZATION MEDITATION

The Polarization Meditation is a simple method to balance your positive and negative energies into harmony. We erroneously think that positive energy is good and negative energy is bad, but they simply refer to an electrical charge. True health and wellbeing come from our energies being in balance, not when one is dominating the other. Witches know through the Hermetic Principle of Polarity that all things must have their poles, their own forms of the positive and negative, and the dynamic balance is what keeps us in harmony. Use this meditation whenever you feel unbalanced or off your center.

Enter into an alpha state. On the screen of your mind, visualize a rod with two spheres at the ends. One end is a positive charge. The other end is a negative charge. Mentally turn the rod around one hundred and eighty degrees. You can even reach out with your hands and physically gesture as you turn the rod. Say to yourself:

I polarize all positive and negative energies that are imbalanced in my mind, brain, and body.

To correct this, I turn this pole (turning the pole mentally and with your gesture).

I have now corrected all negative and positive energies to balance my mind, brain, and body.

So mote it be!

Erase the image of the rod with two spheres, give yourself Total Health Clearance, and count yourself up from alpha level.

POLARIZED BREATHING

Some of the most effective energy balancing exercises are simple breathing exercises. Breath controls the flow of our energy. Yogis and Tai-Chi masters learn to synchronize their breath with their movements, and Witches should learn to do this as well. I learned a lot of my own breathing exercises from the wisdom of the Rosicrucians. One book in particular that was very helpful was *Wisdom of the Mystic Masters* by J. Weed, published in 1974. These two polarity breath exercises come from that book; they are techniques I still use and teach to this day and bring about some pretty amazing and immediate results.

POSITIVE BREATHING

Positive breathing is used to balance a "negative" condition, such as falling into depression and lethargy. Whenever pessimism or a lack of energy occurs, try this breath. It can be repeated in two-hour intervals for chronic conditions, and the earlier you "catch" a situation and begin treatment with this breath, the easier it is to restore balance. Lingering conditions will require more repetition. The two-hour break allows the energy to circulate and rebalance. If you do it too quickly, you'll overload your system.

1. Sit in a comfortable position. Take three deep, easy breaths.

2. Make sure that your hands are on your lap and your feet are squarely on the floor.

3. The index finger, middle finger, and thumb of each hand must be held touching each other in a sort of triangle composed of the first two fingers and thumb.

4. Take a deep breath and hold it to the count of seven. Repeat this process six more times.

5. Put the whole procedure out of your mind.

Negative Breathing

Negative Breathing is used to counterbalance an overly "positive" condition, such as when someone is too euphoric or manic. It is also excellent for the common cold and simple infections. While we tend to think of illness as "negative," the cold symptoms are an outward sign of the immune system's activity as it rids itself of an infection. Negative breathing can help subdue the germs in six to eight hours, restoring balance to the body.

1. Sit comfortably as in the previous treatment.

2. This time your feet should be touching each other, squarely on the floor.

3. Hold your hands in front of your body at chest level, thumb touching thumb and each finger touching its corresponding finger on the other hand.

4. Close your eyes and take a deep breath. Exhale slowly.

5. When the air is completely out of your lungs, hold it for the count of seven.

6. Breathe in and out easily and slowly for five to six seconds until you are again relaxed.

7. Repeat, holding the exhale for the count of five.

8. Repeat this cycle seven times, then stop, breathe normally, and put the entire exercise out of your mind.

DRUID CANDLE MEDITATION

The Druid Candle Meditation is a great way to build focus and concentration, a necessary skill for a Witch. It is also an excellent test to see if you need to use the Polarization Meditation to rebalance your energy. If you can't find your center and stillness, it's good to re-polarize yourself and find that balance within.

Use the Crystal Countdown to enter into alpha. Visualize a white candle in the center of your mind's eye. See a beautiful white candle with a strong flickering flame. Hold the image of the candle perfectly still, aside from the flame dancing upon the candle. Focus all your concentration on the candle and nothing else. Release all wandering thoughts, worries, fears, and distractions from the candle. There is nothing but you and the candle. Hold this image for as long as you can.

If you cannot hold the image without being distracted, use the polarization exercise to balance, conjuring the rod with two spheres. Once you are balanced, release the polarization rod, but keep the candle, and you should be able to keep the image of the candle still and clear again.

When you're done, wipe the image from the screen of your mind and return from alpha.

THE CRYSTAL DOOR MIND TRAVEL MEDITATION

Just as the Apple Meditation is a method to practice bringing things to you upon the mind's screen, the Crystal Door Mind Travel Meditation is a method to practice traveling to other places, to prepare you for journey work where you project your awareness to places in this world or other worlds. We use the image of a crystal door as a portal and travel to it on a 45-degree angle, an angle common in forms of spirit flight and shamanism, to allow us easy and safe travel beyond the perceptions of our body.

While many people would confuse this with an out-of-body experience, your spirit is not leaving your body. This is simply a projection of your mind to perceive a new location. For some, it feels like a daydream. Others feel as if they are really at the new location. Neither is better than the other as long as you get the correct information and experience you need.

Enter into alpha using the Crystal Countdown. Conjure the screen of your mind. Upon it, picture a crystal door at a 45-degree angle, way in the distance. You might only see it as a small dot far away, yet you know it is the crystal door. Feel your energy rise up from your feet and toes, legs, stomach, chest, shoulders, neck, and head. Move towards the door as if you are rising into a tunnel, going up and up. Keep going until you feel yourself traveling at the speed of light, the speed of thought. Focus upon the door as images flash by you on both sides. Do not be distracted by these brain-oriented images. You might even feel pressure on your face as you travel with such speed. You reach the door and know it has the power to take you wherever you want to go.

For your first time, simply observe the door. Look at its colors and its crystalline structure. Now that you know you can reach the door, you can come back with a clear purpose in mind. After getting to know the door and creating a link with it, travel backwards to your starting point, once again with images rushing past you on both sides. You might feel a force upon your back as if you are being pushed or helped back. Return your mind to your bodily awareness. Feel your energy come down through your head, shoulders, stomach, legs, and down into your feet and toes.

Return your awareness to your body, giving yourself Total Health Clearance, and count up from alpha.

Once you know you can connect to the door, start your next meditation with a "flight plan." Before you go, set your intention of what you wish to experience and where you want to project your mind. You can use these skills to explore and investigate a wide range of majickal experiences. In many ways, Witches are explorers of the mind. We can use the Crystal Door to travel anywhere on the Earth and to move forward or backward in time. Many explore foreign jungles and forests. Others visit past civilizations, observing our most ancient ancestors. Seek out past majickal information and find the roots of our stories and myths.

You can investigate other planets and their different dimensions, including layers where worlds that are not ours co-exist with our own dimension. There will be different people, cultures, and societies in that dimension. Some will be familiar to you, while others can be very alien, but regardless, be sure to set an intention of safety and highest good. I once forgot that and explored the planet Mars. I became very dehydrated soon after, not realizing it was triggered by my adventures on Mars. I was left in bed for a week. There are many layers of dimensions to each world, and if I had been wiser, I would have approached Mars from another layer and not had such a physical response in my body.

Write your intention and speak it like a spell, informing the powers of the universe of your plan, and you will be safe and protected. Specify where you wish to explore and that you desire it be for your highest good and have no harm to you. Write it out, speak it before counting down, and hold the list in your physical hand as you travel. You can use this format:

I, (State your Name), ask in the name of the Divine Mind, the Universe, the All, to be granted a safe journey to (fill in the location and/or time period). I ask (fill in any details of how you want the journey to be, including who or what you wish to encounter). I ask this be completely safe and harm none, and be for my highest good. So mote it be.

If you are familiar with crafting potions, you can put a drop of protection potion upon the intention paper. If you are not, but remain concerned about safety, I suggest looking to the Protection Meditations in **Chapter Three** before opening the Crystal Door, to make sure you feel safe and secure.

OUT OF BODY VOYAGE

This meditation prepares you for workings that take you outside of your body. While not a far journey, it is a preparation for other kinds of meditative and psychic work on the etheric level of consciousness.

Sit down on a clean white sheet. Use your hands to touch your feet and your shins. Touch your thighs, your stomach, your chest, and then your arms and shoulders. Be conscious of your physical body. Use your fingertips and touch the sheet on which you are sitting. Feel the fabric of the sheet and be conscious of where you are.

Lie down on the sheet and close your eyes. Visualize in your mind's eye your physical body and the surroundings that you have just touched; see the details of your body and surroundings. Visualize your entire body from your head down to your ankles and see your feet become invisible. From the ankles down, you see the clean white sheet. There is an indentation in the sheet where your heels rest.

Visualize your body once again, from the top of your head and down to your knees. Below the knees, your legs are invisible now, and you can only see the white sheet and the indentation that your calves make in the sheet. There is an indentation where your heels touch the sheet, but your legs from the knees down and your feet are invisible.

Visualize your entire body again from the head down. Visualize down to your waist, and from the waist down, your body is now invisible. You can see the beautiful clean white sheet and the indentation where your body touches the sheet. You are now invisible from the waist down.

In your mind's eye, see your body from the head down. You see your head and face and your chest. Visualize your head, and from the neck down, you are invisible. There is an indentation where your back touches the sheet, but your body now is invisible. Your arms are invisible. Visualize your head and visualize it disappearing now. It has vanished. You are invisible, and all that you can see from your mind's eye is the clean white sheet. You are out of your body now. Your image is standing next to the clean white sheet. Your etheric body is in the room standing next to you, and you can look down at the beautiful white sheet. You are invisible, and you feel good. Turn around 360 degrees in place and look at the room.

(Pause here for seven minutes to explore this experience.)

You are getting used to being out of your body. And when you get good at this, you can walk around and consciously lower the vibration of your etheric body. Say to yourself, "I am comfortable. I feel wonderful. I am free. I am now lowering my body and my etheric body vibration so that I am in more control of my etheric body, so that I can touch matter, and this is so."

(Pause again for seven minutes to explore this experience.)

When you are done, you can return by visualizing the white sheet. Come back to the white sheet. In your mind's eye, visualize the indentation in the sheet where your body rests. See your head, neck, and shoulders return upon the white sheet. Visualize in your mind's eye the return of your arms and body down to your waist. Look at the indentation in the sheet from your lower body, then visualize the return of your body below the waist, the legs and calves, and finally the ankles and feet. Feel yourself resting upon the sheet.

Open your eyes, and use your hands to touch the sheet, then your head and face, shoulders, arms, and chest. Touch your stomach and thighs, then move down to your legs, shins, and finally to your feet. You have returned to your body.

Practice this meditation to experience yourself out of your body.

Chapter 3: Protection Majick

Protection is an important part of your majickal practice. While we like to think the world is a beautiful and safe place, experience shows that it has a mix of forces. Some are helpful and healing. Some can be harmful, intentionally or otherwise. Witches don't seek to attack or do harm, but they do know how to protect themselves from harm by creating powerful shields and filters and by casting protective spells.

Many people fear they will be unsafe when they are doing meditation. Years of religious dogma have made many inherently fear majick and psychic abilities, believing they open you to demonic forces. Nothing could be further from the truth. They are a natural part of who and what you are as a human being. We have simply forgotten their role in our life, and it's the Witch's job to help us remember. As our ancestors knew, majick is as natural as breathing, eating, and sleeping.

We can encounter unfamiliar energies, spirits, and entities that do not understand what humans are. Therefore, we intend for all our work in alpha to be "for the good of all" and "harming none," pre-programming us towards the experiences and events that are for our highest good. Guided meditation uses pre-determined paths that someone has traveled before, leaving guideposts to keep you safe. But we all—from time to time in our visions and in our dreams—explore. Setting up your protection shield and grounding yourself regularly are ways to stay safe and neutralize any potential harm, not only when meditating, but in regular day-to-day life.

PROTECTION SHIELD MEDITATION

The foundation of protection majick in the Cabot Tradition is the protection shield. We establish protection shields around our bodies and spirits, our family, animals, homes, and even when necessary, our friends. We create the protection shield by using the light energy of the aura, shaping it in our mind's eye into an enormous crystal egg. The egg of crystalline light extends all around you, above your head, below your feet, and beyond your reach in all directions. We program the energy to be a shield, to block and ground all harmful, unbalanced energy. The shield really acts as a filter, allowing in the energies you desire, energies that would be helpful and good for you, while stopping anything that would harm you or be incorrect for your life.

The shield taps into the wisdom of the Divine Mind, the All, because sometimes we are not wise enough to know what is harmful. Many things can feel correct to us, based on our societal programming and unconscious desires. We can sabotage ourselves and invite harmful energies and people into our lives. The shield helps to minimize this experience. While it doesn't stop physical harm the way a majickal shield in a movie or television might—which is why you should always take common sense precautions in addition to majickal ones—it does heighten your intuition and perception, naturally guiding you out of many harmful situations and circumstances. The shield will alert you (often unconsciously) to dangers and draw you to circumstances out of harm's way.

Unless you purposely deconstruct it, the shield is permanent, but can be renewed to build its strength over time. Wise Witches will renew it as a part of their regular meditation practice or when going through difficult times in life and their spiritual development.

Enter into an alpha state and reach your innermost level. Envision yourself inside a giant crystalline egg that shields you from all harm. The crystal shield is forming around you now, the crystal light extending beyond the reach of your fingertips. You can see the sparkling crystal light around you. Your protection shield is in the shape of an egg, enclosing your feet, head, hands, and body. You are completely enclosed by your shield.

Once the shield is formed, look at it carefully. It is like looking through a crystal ball or a faceted quartz crystal. There are inclusions in real crystals and in your protection shield. It does not have to be only pure white or clear light; it can also be a mixture of colors. Take a good look at it. Feel the energy and the protection.

Sit within your crystal light. Enjoy the safety and comfort of the crystal shield.

While you are resting in your shield, you are going to repeat in your mind:

"This shield will protect me from all negative and positive energies and forces that may come to do me harm.

This shield will protect me from all negative and positive energies and forces that may come to do me harm.

This shield will protect me from all negative and positive energies and forces that may come to do me harm.

This shield is fixed. And it is so."

These words will help the brain draw in the energy to establish the shield. Words direct your consciousness to perform a task.

In your mind's eye, with your intention, explore the shield around you. Hold your hand out in front of you to test the shield's distance. You want to put your hands above you and see how far up it goes. How far beyond your hand does it go? Put your hands straight down beside you and see how far below your feet it goes. Enjoy and rest in your protection shield.

When you are done, give yourself Total Health Clearance and count yourself up from alpha level to waking consciousness.

Once the shield is established, you will be able to sense it even when you are not in meditation. You can reach out with your hand and feel the energy. If you work majickally with others, you'll find everyone sees their own shield, and yours, a little bit differently, based upon their personal perceptions of energy. This is totally normal, so don't be alarmed by it. Be confident your shield is established and working. Periodically you can check it, reinforcing it by repeating this meditation, and over time, your own perceptions of it might change.

Regardless if you remember your shield, it is working for you. If you do recall it, your memory of it in difficult times can strengthen it, but mostly we forget about it and let it work throughout our day.

While it does use the energy of the aura, it's good to understand that it is not the aura itself. Your aura contains all your life energy information, and it will fluctuate with your mood, circumstances, and astrology. The shield is directed, programmed, and clear. The shield can help us process information, but ultimately it is the aura that is the force receiving, directing, and sending the energy of our lives.

When you feel you have a strong understanding of shielding, you can also repeat this meditation, and rather than shielding yourself, you can place the shield around anyone or anything important to you. You simply envision the person or object in need of shielding upon the screen of your mind and form the crystal egg around them as you did for yourself. Program it with similar words. Ideally you should ask permission of other adults before shielding them, though parents should help shield their own children. You can put a shield around not only your car, but any vehicle you ride in. I do it when I get into someone else's car. I don't like to fly, so when I'm in an airplane, I put a shield around the whole plane.

WHITE LIGHT PENTACLES

A powerful method of protection found in many traditions is the drawing of pentagrams (five-pointed stars) or pentacles (five-pointed stars in circles) in colored light around anything you wish to protect. I use pentacles drawn in white light as shields and filters.

Fig. 1: Pentacle

The pentacle is a symbol of the Witch, but it is also a sign of universal wisdom and protection. It acts much like a cosmic circuit board, directing divine wisdom. It directs information in alignment with the divine mind. Traditionally a sign of sacred geometry and the ancient teachings of Pythagoras, a pentagram's five points are symbolic of the five senses, with the circle as the sixth psychic sense. The points also represent the five elements of earth, air, fire, water, and spirit. All things are made from the five elements in combination. It is also a symbol of humanity, with the body of two arms, two legs, and the head making five points. Old grimoires would depict a man outstretched upon the pentacle. The pentacle in Tarot is often known as the coin and is a symbol of elemental earth and prosperity, but in other Tarot and majickal traditions, it is known as the shield, for it protects you.

You can use the following meditation to supplement your personal protection shield:

> Enter into an alpha state. Direct your majick by using your mind's eye and draw a white light pentacle above your protection shield. Repeat with a second below your protection shield. Then place one in each of the four directions—before you, to your right, behind you, and to your left. Now you are protected even beyond the edge of your protection shield. State that these pentacles are to protect from all harm, and these shields are fixed.

Once you feel comfortable creating the white light pentacles, you can use the same techniques to create them at the doors and windows of your home, on the four outside walls of the building, and on the roof and basement. They will protect you from harm like a shield. Whenever you need some extra protection, you can envision and create a pentacle of protection in white light.

THE ROSICRUCIAN PROTECTION ARROW

Other symbols—such as Celtic knots, the Ogham alphabet, Nordic runes, and Egyptian hieroglyphs—can be used for protection majick, and while more commonly used in charms and spells, they can be envisioned and empowered in white light. One of the most powerful and simple ˌsymbols I learned was from Master Thomas, my friend from the Rosicrucian Lodge in Arlington, Massachusetts. He taught me many things complementary to my Witchcraft, but in particular, he helped me deal with hate mail and threats from more conservative Christians as I became more well known as a local Witch. He used this double-arrow symbol for protection.

Fig. 2: Rosicrucian Double Arrow

When feeling particularly attacked from outside forces, whether human or spiritual, you can enter into an alpha state and envision this double arrow of protection in all directions, preventing harm from coming to you.

WHITE LIGHT DRAGONS

Dragons are mysterious and powerful creatures, ones we will explore further in the chapter on Avalon. And while there are dragons of the earth and the sky, we can also shape and program energy to form powerful images, and I use the image of a dragon.

Once you know how to create images in white light, such as the pentacles of protection, you can expand upon that skill and use white light to create other forms and program them with intention. I have created two dragons of white light. They touch tail to tail around my home, with the heads guarding the entrance. They are generally appearing as if they are asleep, but if someone enters the area with ill intentions, they wake up and protect my home, frightening away any would-be attacker.

In some majickal traditions, such images are known as thought form constructs or artificial elementals, but they are much more than that. They are not just made of thought, but also of light and pure energy. They can incorporate elemental energy, but they are really drawn from the psychic light of the universal mind. They are not really dragon spirits, with their own will and direction, but energetic constructs, programmed by intention and governed by their shape and nature to fulfill a purpose.

Before creating a white light dragon, be clear in your intention. I think they work best for protection, though theoretically you can ask them to do anything. Shop owners might draw in more customers or healers might ask for a peaceful healthy environment. But the nature of dragons is fierce, so they do best warding away harm, not unlike the gargoyles found on cathedrals or the dog-like guardians in Buddhist temples.

Most people anchor the white light dragon to their home, office, or vehicle. Some conjure white light dragons to act like familiars, protecting their Witch while in meditation and traveling in vision. Just be clear in your intention. You can even write it out like a spell, to make sure your instructions are exactly what you want them to be.

Go into a meditative state. On the screen of your mind, create the image of a dragon entirely of white light. With each moment, add more detail. How large is it? What kind of body? Does it have wings? How many legs? Does your dragon breathe fire? What do the face, the mouth, and the teeth look like? Craft a realistic dragon image, sculpted in white light.

Instruct your dragon. What do you want it to do? Be clear in your instructions. Then place the dragon where it is to operate. Envision it wrapping around your house, your car, or anywhere else appropriate for its work.

When you are done, give yourself Total Health Clearance and return from alpha.

Like protection shields, periodically check in and renew the meditation to strengthen the dragon. Don't be surprised if others who are psychically sensitive will sense that something is different, or even feel the presence of the dragon.

While dragons are my favorite image, you can use other figures to the same effect. I have had a student who put sleeping wolves on her roof that will come down and scare away harmful people. Another uses unicorns, which might seem cute, but mythologically have always been fierce and powerful creatures.

GOLDEN RING AND STAR OF PROTECTION

This is a simple protection visualization that doesn't require a deep trance.

Stand in a place where you have space enough on the floor around you to visualize a circle nine feet in diameter with you in the center. Envision golden flame coming out of your fingers. Use this fire like a beam of light to draw a five-pointed star on the floor, top point before you, so you are in the center of the pentagram. Then draw a clockwise circle around the star, forming a pentacle on the floor in golden fire with you in the center. Recite this incantation:

A golden ring
Around a star
Will keep me safe
Hour by hour.
So shall it be!

Envision the golden light of divine intelligence rising up around you and protecting you from all harm by neutralizing unwanted energies and guiding you to be in the right place at the right time.

Let the vision fade but know the golden energy still travels with you, giving you an additional layer of protection.

Chapter 4: Energy Work & Healing Meditations

Entering an alpha state improves your health, lowers your blood pressure, and promotes peace within you. With the addition of a little conscious attention and some focused breath, you can also control and direct the life force energy of your body. This life force is known by many names, including *chi, ki,* and *prana.* Martial arts use movement and breath to improve the flow of this energy. By shifting your energy, you can heal specific parts of your body, remove blocks, and expand your conscious awareness.

Different mystical systems map out the flow of energy in the body. In India, they describe seven main energy centers called *chakras* (often depicted as flowers) as well as paths known as *nadis* and three central channels running parallel to the spine. Chinese medicine outlines acupuncture points and meridian lines, corresponding to the major organs and bodily systems. In Jewish mysticism the energy centers correspond with points on the Tree of Life. The Celts might have described major energy points as three cauldrons.

Use these meditations to manage and shift your personal life force. Add the connections made in the meditation to rejuvenate and heal.

THE PINK STAR JOURNEY

One of my favorite meditations is the Pink Star Meditation. Pink light is the light of self-esteem. When we experience the vibration of the color pink, we open ourselves to self-love. It can transform our current mood, but over time, it can alter our overall attitudes, including the subtle ways we experience ourselves and others, because we are experiencing everything from a place of love.

While you can send yourself pink light anytime—and in the short term, it can help with a bad day, depression, or general pessimism—you can journey to the pink star to truly focus upon self-love and infuse your aura with the energy of self-esteem. Through the pink star, you can clear your own mind and emotions, removing all the blocks to happiness and success. Some of these blocks are created by others, and we have accepted them. Others we have created ourselves, but in either case, pink light can help us dissolve and dismantle them. The preparation for the Pink Star Journey is a chakra-balancing meditation, aligning you with the powers, the stars, within your own body. Then you will be ready to journey to the pink star and receive its full benefit.

> Lie down upon your bed or couch and get comfortable. Use the Crystal Countdown method to enter into an alpha meditative state. Envision the sky above you. Experience the wonder of the cosmos. Above you are the lights of the universe, and through those lights, the blessings of the God and the Goddess of the All.

> White light descends from the cosmos and appears down at your feet. The large ball of white light encompasses your feet. Within the ball of light is a red light emanating from a red stone. The red stone empowers you and heals your body. It fills your cells with life force and power.

The light moves up to your belly to what is known as the spleen chakra. In the center of the white light is now an orange stone, radiating an orange light. It empowers you. You feel safe.

The light moves up to your solar plexus. In the center of the ball of white light is a yellow stone, shining with a yellow energy. You feel powerful and strong with the light glowing at your solar plexus.

The light moves up now to your ribcage, to your heart. Within the ball of light is a green light, shining from a green emerald. The heart opens, and you feel love and empathy.

The light moves now to your throat. In the center of the light at your throat is a blue stone shining with a bright blue light. Your mind feels peaceful and clear.

Soon the light rises to your brow, to the place of your third eye. Here is your mind's eye. The white light now contains a purple or indigo stone. The dark purple light awakens your third eye, so you can receive psychic light and send it from the brow.

With the previous six points energized, the light rises to the crown. Within the white ball of light is a stone of orchid light, radiating outward and granting a sense of spiritual connection. A crown forms on your head, like a many-petalled flower.

The flower begins to move and turn and spin. The flower, like a lotus, rises above the crown, up above you. It floats swiftly upward, as if seeking the surface of a lake. Let your consciousness float with the flower, upward and onward.

Travel beyond the Earth and Moon. Travel into the solar system. Travel past all the planets, into the stars.

The flower of your consciousness goes way beyond known space. Keep going until you see the mysterious pink star. Its rays of pink light extend outward in all directions. The flower of your consciousness brings you to the pink star. The gravity of the star brings you closer and closer. Let its rays strike you, filling you with the light of self-esteem and self-love. Bathe yourself in it. Fill yourself with it. Make every fiber of your being radiate with pink light.

The power of the star draws you into the star itself. You find yourself one with the entire cosmos, the Goddess, the God, the Divine Mind, the All.

You reach out and grab two large "handfuls" of light. You carry this light and the petals of the flower star out of the star and back into space. You float through space, following the way you journeyed to the star, through the stars of our galaxy, into our solar system, past the Moon, and back to the Earth.

Come back to your body and reenter your physical body from the crown of your head. Feel your energy sink from the crown to the brow, throat, heart, solar plexus, spleen, and down to the feet. In your hands is the pink light from the star. Think about two people with whom you'd like to share this gift of self-love. Picture these two people on the screen of your mind. Take one handful and speak aloud the name of the first recipient. Place the pink light inside this vision of the person's solar plexus and watch the pink light spread in the body and through the aura. Then speak the name of the second person. Place the pink light in your vision of the person, inside their solar plexus, and likewise watch the pink energy spread.

When you are ready, give yourself Total Health Clearance and count up. Affirm you are filled with self-esteem, self-love, and self-confidence, and that you can easily give and accept love.

You can give the gift of pink light not only to people, but to your home. You can fill rooms with it when you return from the star. You can also "paint" your lightbulbs pink with this psychic light, so when you have them on, they will continue to radiate the majickal vibration of self-love.

THE THREE CAULDRONS

A simple understanding of our energy body divides our life force into three major zones. The first is in the belly. The second is in the chest. The third is in the head. You can see this division in some forms of energy healing from Traditional Chinese Medicine; it is suspected that the ancient Celts knew of them and that this knowledge was veiled in an Irish text known as *The Cauldron of Posey*:

"What then is the root of poetry and every other wisdom? Not hard; three cauldrons are born in every person—the Cauldron of Incubation, the Cauldron of Motion, and the Cauldron of Wisdom."

Location	Traditional Name	English Translation	Powers
Belly	*Coire Goiriath*	Cauldron of Incubation (or Warming)	Life Force and Vitality
Heart	*Coire Ermae*	Cauldron of Motion	Heart, Emotions, and Blessings
Head	*Coire Sois*	Cauldron of Wisdom	Enlightenment and Inspiration

Everyone is born with the first cauldron upright and filled, as this is the life force. Most people have the second cauldron tilted on its side, meaning their heart is not fully open. The chest cauldron requires great joy or great sorrow to tip upright. Once it does, the heart opens, and the cauldron can fill up. Turning the third cauldron requires the work of the two upright cauldrons, plus inspiration from the gods (known as *awen* to the Welsh and *imbas* to the Irish). Once it is turned, our full spiritual powers are experienced.

Breathe deep in and out, down into your belly, to feel the lower cauldron. As you breathe, begin relaxing your body from the torso and belly up through the chest and then into the shoulders, neck, and head. Be aware of the three cauldrons—a large energy center in the belly, a second energy center in the heart, and a final energy center in the head. Be aware of these three points of power.

Inhale through the nose and breathe in the energy of the Earth beneath you. Draw that energy up into the belly cauldron. Fill the belly with life force. Sense the warmth growing within you. Keep breathing deeply until the cauldron is filled with energy and you feel revitalized.

On the next inhale, drawn the energy up to your heart center. Allow the energy to trigger great emotion, or the memory of very emotional times, usually points of great joy or great sorrow. The emotion gently rocks the heart and opens the cauldron to its full power. Through an open heart, you feel the self-esteem, love, and compassion of the heart. Keep breathing deeply until you feel the heart cauldron fill up.

When you are ready, breathe deep and draw up the power of the heart. Let the energy of creativity build up until you start to feel a tingling sensation or subtle heat. As the energy builds, you might feel it turn upright, filling your head with divine light and inspiration. The light flows from the top of the skull downward, revitalizing your body and filling the cauldrons below, creating a circulation of energy from the belly, heart, and head, back down to the belly again. You can tap into this creative energy to fulfill your goals and dreams.

When you are done, let the flow of energy fade from your awareness and open your eyes.

THE EGYPTIAN SUN

The Sun is the foremost symbol of the sacred for the ancient Egyptians. It is the source of life and spirit. The Egyptians had many Sun gods, including Ra, Sehkmet, and Horus. Even if we don't work directly with the Egyptian gods, we can borrow the wisdom of ancient Egypt. We can connect to that source of life and spirit through the Egyptian Sun meditation, an energy-based working to restore vitality and life force. The effect of it is like being out in the Sun, but much quicker and longer lasting, as we are drawing the energy into our body, into our vital centers.

Use this meditation to rejuvenate your physical and psychic power.

Enter into a light meditative state by using alpha or simply relaxing into it. Make sure you are sitting up straight and not lying down for this work. Sit in the Egyptian goddess position, with your hands, palm upward, shoulder level, with your fingers facing away from you. Touch your feet together. You will look like a statue of an Egyptian god upon a throne.

When you are relaxed yet focused, become aware of the Sun above your head. Visualize the Sun above you, regardless of the time of day or where the physical Sun is. This is the Sun behind the Sun, the spiritual Sun and true power the Egyptians honored, which is available to us at any time. Feel the light and heat radiating down upon your crown and your whole body.

The Sun begins to flare and stream down beams of light into your body.

The first ray of the Egyptian Sun streams into your crown and directly into your pineal gland.

The second ray streams down into your thyroid gland at your neck.

The third ray flows down into your heart and the thymus gland at the heart.

The fourth ray moves down into your solar plexus and adrenal glands.

The fifth ray enters into the upright palm of your right hand.

The sixth ray likewise enters into the upright palm of your left hand.

Your body and energy system are filling with golden life force, pulsating with it. It flows into all your body systems, restoring their natural health and vigor. Each cell accepts a portion of golden light and strength. As your body fills, you'll feel a tingling sensation all over, particularly in your hands and feet, fingers and toes. When you feel this tingling warmth in your extremities, the meditation is almost complete. Cross your hands and place them over the heart like an Egyptian mummy, forming the Egyptian god position. The flow of light stops, and the light within you will be contained and processed by your body. You will enjoy health, strength, and well-being.

HEALING THE WORLD

This meditation can be used when there is strife and conflict in the world. While it is easy to feel powerless, Witches know we are never powerless. Take a situation in the world that is distressing for you, that you feel needs to be healed. If you can get something tangible, like a newspaper article on the topic, that is great. Make use of various news sources, from global resources beyond your home country, particularly for Americans who need to have a more global view of world problems. Become educated about the issue to the best of your ability and hold it in your mind.

When you are ready, count down into alpha. Intend to connect to the wisdom of the Divine Mind, the All. Envision on the screen of your mind the situation or issue. Please pick only one issue at a time, or one aspect of a large issue, rather than trying to face all the world's problems at once. If there are leaders involved whose actions and decisions could shift the situation for the better, ask the Divine Mind to speak to the leaders involved. Use your own inner voice (regardless of any language barriers as you are using pure thought and intention) and speak to the leaders. Ask them to discontinue their policies of destruction and engage in the policies and actions that will bring the greatest good. Ask them to find the peaceful solution. Then thank them, even if you are unsure if they agreed.

Ask to go to those who are being harmed, or to the other side of the conflict if both sides are causing harm. Repeat your previous action. If anyone on either side requires protection, place a protection shield around them.

Ask the divine power of the universe that all those in need in the situation get what they need, be it food, clothing, shelter, medicine, or anything else. Ask this for the good of all involved. Visualize the situation coming to a peaceful resolution. Thank the Divine Mind.

Give yourself Total Health Clearance and bring yourself out of alpha. Ground yourself as needed.

Repeat as you feel called to do so, as you would for any other healing, but don't get too stuck or fixated. You can contribute to the solution, but you are not the sole source of the solution. Make sure you rest for a few days before repeating this meditation or choosing another situation to work on. This process can be quite difficult, so pace yourself and take care of yourself.

Chapter 5: Meditations for Life

Majick is not always about the deep mysteries. It can also be practical, a tool to help us in our daily life. People seek the Witch out to get help with their needs and wants, and many Witches study Witchcraft to do it for themselves. Throughout history, people have sought out the Witch for help with prosperity, love, healing, and happiness. These meditations can help with life's needs and desires, manifesting them from a place of balance and clear purpose.

THE MAJICK MIRROR

While not quite a deep meditation, the Majick Mirror exercise is one of the key practices of an aspiring Witch in the Cabot Tradition. It's easy to do, and while at first you might feel foolish, it can be fun.

When you get up in the morning, as you are performing your daily hygiene routine, gaze at yourself in the mirror. When you're ready, say

I love you.

Allow yourself to give and receive love, the root of self-esteem. Follow it up with these affirmations:

You are wonderful.

You deserve the very best.

Repeat this practice every day. If you feel self-conscious, put on some morning music to prevent your household from hearing you, but you must speak these things out loud to yourself. Spoken words have power. Everyone feels foolish or strange doing this at first, but after a few weeks, it won't bother you anymore. I've found that people look forward to it, knowing that at least one person, their very own self, is their cheerleader, and they actually miss it if they forget.

You can make your own special Witch's Mirror or Majick Mirror, a dark mirror that can be used not only for self-esteem work—reminding us to look at the shadow, at the unacknowledged and unloved parts of ourselves--but also for scrying and as a portal, a majick doorway, into other realms. You will need:

Any Glass Photo Frame and Glass
Black Spray Paint
Sprinkle Glitter
Parchment Paper
Tea Stain and Brush
Glue
Eyebright
Rosemary
Chamomile
Frankincense
Myrrh

Start with a picture frame that has an arm on the back so it can be freestanding. You want something you can place on an altar or table and gaze into, without worrying about getting so deep into trance that you drop the mirror. Next, powder all the herbs as fine as you possibly can, using your mortar and pestle or an electric grinder used only for majick. Spray paint one side of the glass in the frame with black spray paint. Then, as it is drying, sprinkle it with silver and/or gold glitter. Sprinkle the herbs into the paint with the glitter. The frankincense and myrrh are used to neutralize and protect you from anything false coming through the mirror, the eyebright and chamomile help you psychically see, and the rosemary helps you remember all that you've seen. They are all herbs of the Sun, its light shining through the dark mirror.

Write on the parchment the following verse:

Mirror mirror
show to me,
all the good things
that can be.

Or

Mirror mirror
let me see,
all the good things
that will come to be.

Tea-stain the edges of the parchment. Then glue the parchment on the back of the mirror to seal the enchantment. Set it out under the full Moon, making sure to bring it in before the Sun rises, and keep it covered with a dark cloth when not using it. When it is ready, unveil the mirror and gaze into it for majickal work. The mirror can also be used like the Crystal Door.

PROSPERITY MEDITATION

Part of the work of the Witch is to balance our spiritual and material needs, finding our wealth in both the spiritual and material planes of existence. Neither extreme wealth nor extreme poverty is balanced. Money can be quite a stressful issue for many of us, but with an understanding of consciousness, money should not be a problem, and we should certainly not stress over it as we do in our modern society. Everyone is entitled to a level of personal prosperity, having their needs and wants met, and the secret to prosperity is changing our consciousness around it. Our own limiting beliefs and thoughts can prevent us from creating prosperity.

Light a candle in one of the colors of Jupiter, the planet of good fortune. Jupiter's colors are royal blue, purple, and turquoise. Go into a meditative state by breathing deeply and relaxing your body. Envision yourself surrounded by royal blue, purple, and turquoise, the colors swirling around you. As you breathe in, your breath is the colors of Jupiter. As you breathe out, breathe out all blocks to your own prosperity and good fortune. The light of Jupiter just breaks them apart.

While breathing in the light, recite these affirmations in your mind. Like seeds, feel them become planted in your mind and start to grow. These seeds will bear the fruits of prosperity for years to come if you care for them through repeated use of the meditation.

Money enables me to obtain the goods and services I need and helps provide these services to the world.

Money is an acceptable form of exchange throughout the world.

I create my own financial situation.

I deserve prosperity.

Imagine yourself successful, having both material and spiritual wealth. What would that look like? How would you feel when you are successful? Conjure a new image of your success and become one with it, as if it is happening to you right now. Enjoy this feeling for as long as you want.

When you are done, breathe deep again, to take that majick into you. Then bring your awareness back to the world around you. Snuff out the candle, and when you repeat this meditation, relight it. Keep doing this meditation until the candle burns out to make sure you've planted and watered the seeds of prosperity with your intention.

LOVE MEDITATION

Traditionally Witches are said to be blessed in love. I am not sure if that's always true, but people often seek majick because they are seeking love. We know that true love has to start from within, so to begin this meditation, build an altar of all the material things that you really love. Use things that you absolutely love to look at and think about, items that give you joy. This helps viscerally conjure the power of self-love, as those objects are a part of your love of self, and that love will help draw a physical partner, a love interest, to you. Everyone is entitled to love and romance if it is their desire. Part of our block to such love is not feeling worthy of receiving it.

Amid the altar of love items, place a green candle for Venus, the planet of love and romance. Light the candle and gaze upon the items. Feel the love. Then enter into a meditative state of alpha. Envision yourself surrounded by the items you love, and by vibrant green light. As you breathe in, you breathe in the color of Venus. As you breathe out, you breathe out all the blocks to your own love and romance. The light of Venus clears and heals you.

Call upon the Goddess of Love, any goddess you feel strongly is a goddess of love for you. You could call upon Maeve or Mab. Isis is well known for her deep and lasting love for Osiris. Ostara is the lady love of the Sun King, and with her associations with rabbits and fertility, would be an excellent choice for a love leading to marriage and a family.

Feel the presence of the goddess as a shadow in the green light of Venus. Feel her with you, stepping out of the green light before you. The goddess reaches towards you and places her hand upon your heart. She blesses you. She blesses you with love and draws the correct and right lover to come to you. Feel the presence of the hidden lover in the green light. How do you feel with your new love? Let that feeling flow through you as the goddess blesses the union of the two of you coming together.

The Goddess of Love gives you a kiss on the cheek and says farewell, fading back into the green light.

Breathe deep and let this energy circulate within you. Return to normal breathing and bring your awareness back to the world around you. Let the candle burn as long as you can and snuff it out as necessary, relighting it and letting it eventually burn all the way down. Be on the lookout for the lover that is right for you.

INNER CHILD HEALING MEDITATION

One of the most important parts of our healing journey is working on our relationship with our parents. Parents provide the biggest influence on our young lives, and they set a foundation that can be both healing and harming, even with the most loving parents. People in our society are not taught to be good parents and do harm without knowing any better. When parents haven't done any introspective work for themselves, they pass on generational issues they are not even conscious they possess. I was the same way, though I didn't realize it until I publicly embraced my Witchcraft and moved to Salem with two young girls. I loved my parents very much, but I realized that some of their upbringing was harming me. I didn't want to pass it onto my daughters.

This meditation is a great one for helping us re-pattern our childhood experience with our parents. I have found it helpful for so many students. Majickally, you become your own parent, taking responsibility for your child self.

Relax yourself and enter into a deeper state of awareness. Go through your entire body, just as a baby does, exploring itself. Start by relaxing your toes. Move up to your legs, relaxing them, feeling your body releasing any tension and returning to a primal state of innocence. Relax the belly. Adults hold a lot of tension in their belly, but children do not. Relax your chest. Feel your arms, hands, and fingers relax. Release tension in your neck and head. Breathe deep and relax your mind. Let go of all your worries and cares. Return to that joy. Through that joy and innocence, we turn back time.

Travel back to a time in your childhood, a birthday you remember. Your adult self is now looking on, like a guest, upon the birthday scene. Look around and see who is there. Look at whatever is going on. What do you see? Find yourself, your child self, at your birthday.

Walk up to your child self, hold out your hand, and say to your child self, *"I am your parent now. I want you to come with me."*

You take your past self's hand and walk out of the celebration room. You continue to walk together, walking out of the house. You hold hands tightly until you walk out and around the corner, leaving behind any view of the old house.

You sit down, and your child self is standing before you, directly in front of you.

Gaze deeply into your child's eyes and say, *"I am your parent now. I love you. I'm going to take care of you. I won't let anyone harm you."*

Look at your child. Notice your face when you were young. Look at the sincerity, the love and care of your child self. Hold out your arms to bring your child self toward you lovingly. Embrace each other and repeatedly whisper into the child's ear, *"I love you. I'm going to take care of you. I'll never let anyone harm you again."*

With your heart and mind, with your majick, hold the child within you. You have become the parent to this little person within you. This child is an important part of you and your well-being. Hold the child within your Witch's heart.

While in vision, cross your physical arms across your chest, touching your own physical body. As you do, you are touching the child within you. Feel the love you have for each other. Nurture your inner child.

When you are done, return your awareness from your heart to your entire body, once again being aware of your fingers and toes, ankles and wrists. Bring your awareness back to the here and now, yet always keep the child in your heart.

THE FOREST OF MYSTERY

The forest is a great teacher to me. I've learned many lessons from walking in the woods and communing with the trees and animals. I've visited the ancient woods in my dreams, and I have returned to the forest in my meditations. While you can count in and out of alpha for this meditation, I often experience it more like a daydream, simply by closing and opening my eyes.

Relax. Breathe deep and close your eyes. The moment you close your eyes, you see the wind swaying the tall pine trees. Breathe in and smell the wafting scent of the clean fresh pine coming from the trees. As you continue to breathe in and out, the pine scent contrasts with the rich earth smell from the ferns and other plants on the forest floor. You realize you are by the forest of mysteries, and you follow a gentle path deeper as you gaze at the dance of the trees.

With each step, you feel the strong earth beneath you. Each step you take is balanced and healthy.

Walk deeper into the mysterious woods. There the world of all the elements is alive. The plants and trees are from the earth. The wind moves through the branches and touches your cheek. A simple stream runs through the forest, forming pools that swirl and flow.

The animals gather in a small clearing in the forest. They come to greet you. What kinds of animals are there to visit you?

Animals make sounds to welcome, and when necessary, to warn. They are aware of the invisible world all around us. It is not a world to fear, but another kind of beauty not seen by those who do not hear the voice of nature first. Feel the presence of the spirits of the forest, the spirits of nature, gathered around the plants and trees. What do you sense?

The birds chirp loudly, and the squirrels chatter, making you aware of the forest once again. Yet the invisible world is always around you.

A sudden breeze wraps around your legs and upward, blowing the branches above you. The canopy opens, allowing a ray of sunlight to beam down through the twilight onto the forest floor. What does the light reveal upon the ground? Is it a special animal, plant, or stone? What does it mean to you?

Far ahead in the woods, you hear sounds like children at play. You glimpse in the distance what strangely appears to be a baby bear in a red coat, playing by itself in the woods. How is that possible? Is the bear alone? Or is it playing with invisible friends? Can you go visit with the bear and play with it?

The bear will lead you through the forest. Journey with this strange bear and its invisible friends. It reminds you of a circus bear, and you realize that perhaps it is the spirit of a baby bear who has passed and who now resides in this forest as a spirit. Learn about playfulness from the bear.

Eventually the bear leads you out of the forest of mystery. Say farewell. Gaze back up at the pine trees. Watch them sway in the breeze. Bring your awareness back to yourself. When you are ready, open your eyes.

Chapter 6: Animal Spirits

Animals are powerful allies of the Witch.. The stereotype of the Witch with her black cat is not far off. Many Witches, myself included, have kept black cats as majickal allies. Animals can act as our familiars as we develop deep majickal relationships with them, our bond benefitting our mutual development. Your familiar doesn't have to be a cat, though cats are excellent psychics themselves. Dogs, birds, rabbits, and snakes can make excellent familiars and household companions, each with traditional majick associations. These friends can help open us to new levels of animal majick.

Witches work with the animal powers as teachers and healers. We honor their place in nature. Sometimes we call upon them as the four elemental guardians of our circle, choosing animal spirits that resonate naturally with the elements in question. We also encounter the animal powers in meditation and spiritual journey. Many goddesses and gods are associated with specific types of animals or take the shape of those animals, which gives us a clue to the deity's power. Likewise, the deity gives us an understanding of the animal's own nature.

We can learn the art of shapeshifting from inner-world animal allies. To shapeshift is to take on another form. Celtic myth and lore are filled with many different forms of shapeshifting, particularly found in the popular translations of the Irish text known as *The Song of Amergin.* In all majickal cultures, practitioners and healers would take on the form of animals to embody their specific powers, particularly in healing rituals. People mistakenly think this is meant to happen in the physical body, and since that concept seems ridiculous to the modern person, the very idea of shapeshifting is dismissed. But the shift is occurring in our spiritual bodies. Our energy body can take on the characteristics of an animal, or several animals. Such a transformation grants us the perspective and powers of those animals.

When we take on the shape of one animal energetically, the animal becomes a vehicle for us to travel to other places and lands. The animal shape is like a cloak for our awareness when we travel astrally into other realms, or when we practice remote viewing. The skills of the animal become a part of us, so animals with keen senses will help perceive things more clearly on a psychic level. Medieval Witches traditionally traveled in the form of birds such as owls and crows, or across the land as hares.

The story of Taliesin and Cerridwen with a shapeshifting chase gives us an understanding of this majick through the four elements. Taliesin, as the boy Gwion Bach, becomes a hare, a salmon, a wren, and then moves outside of the animal realm to become a grain of corn. The goddess Cerridwen becomes a greyhound, an otter, a hawk, and then a black hen to eat the grain.

We seek the wisdom of our ancestors by learning to commune with, and take the shape of, our sacred animal allies. Let them be teachers and healers to you.

THE CAT

The cat is the traditional familiar of the Witch. Cats are majickal creatures, spending much of their time in the alpha state, giving them an awareness of things unseen by humans. Cats can be guides, healers, and protectors. You don't need to have a cat in your home to evoke the majick of the cat spirit. You can commune with the cat in meditation and ask for its protection and aid.

Light a black candle. If you happen to have any cat fur as a majickal ingredient for your spells, place some in a small charm bag and hold it in your left hand. Get comfortable in your chair. Unlike other meditations where I would recommend you sit up straight and have your feet on the floor, for this one, move like a cat, in whatever way is comfortable for you. You can curl up, lie down, or position yourself in any other way you think would be appropriate. Recite this spell for calling upon the cat spirit:

Feline form fierce and pretty,
keep me from harm.
I call your name.
Blessed be!

Stretch and relax your body. Release all tension. Close your eyes. Settle into a meditative, daydream-like state. Feel yourself enter into a dark shadowy place. The time is night, and the air is cool upon your skin. As you look up, you see the soft glow of the Moon above you, guiding you. Your eyes settle and the path becomes clear. You begin to casually walk the path, not really knowing where you are going, and soon you hear the soft sound of a "meow" in the distance. You follow the sound. It is as if the cat is calling to you.

Soon you turn a corner, and there waiting for you is the spirit of the cat. What kind of cat is meeting with you? What color is its fur? Is it tame or wild? How old is it? This cat is a guardian and protector.

It begins to walk away, and you know you are bidden to follow it. You soon feel as if you are shape-shifting into a cat yourself, and you follow the moves of this spirit teacher mimicking what it does, so you can learn the ways of the cat.

The cat spirit leads you on an adventure into her world, daring you to see things through the eyes of a cat. Follow the path and learn what you can about the mystery of the cat.

When done, you'll find that your own form is taking shape again, leaving behind the form of the cat. You shift your shape back into the form of a human and say farewell to your cat teacher. Let the vision fade and return your awareness to the world around you. Get up from your comfortable position, give yourself Total Health Clearance, and return to the waking world.

THE FLIGHT OF THE OWL

Owls are majickal night birds associated with Witches and goddesses. Most people misunderstand them, as they have many different spiritual meanings, depending on the culture. Owls have a divine feminine power that is often distorted and misunderstood. Many consider an owl crossing your path an omen of misfortune or even death.

Most popular and well-known of mythic owls is the Greek goddess Athena's owl of wisdom. Owls are associated with the rebellious figure of Lilith, the first wife of Adam in a non-Biblical story of the Garden of Eden. Less well-known is the owl goddess Blodeuwedd. She begins her journey as a flower maiden, crafted by the Welsh gods Gwydion and Math. This flower goddess was turned into an owl by Gwydion's majick as punishment for betraying and plotting the death of his nephew, Lleu. The feathers of an owl's face are said to be like blooming flowers.

The blessings of owl are silent flight, which lends to its air of secrecy. As nightbirds, they see a whole different world, with keen night vision. They have the unusual ability to turn their necks almost all the way around, giving them a perception of the world that most of us lack, adding to their wisdom and otherworldliness. Owls are excellent hunters. Like many birds, after swallowing their prey, they regurgitate the undigested parts as a mass, called an owl pellet, including bones, fur, feathers, claws, beak, teeth, and the exoskeletons of insects. They can teach us to how to release the things that are not good for us to take in and digest, whether emotionally, spiritually, or majickally.

Owls make an excellent spiritual vehicle to travel to otherworlds and perform remote viewing. They lend us their vision, and like some of the burrowing animals, they can help us see what we normally can't see in our lives and environment. Their silent glide can also help us learn the arts of stealth and invisibility, useful when we don't want to be detected in a natural setting or during psychic travel.

Owl feathers are technically illegal to own in the United States, so many people connect with owl using a photo, statue, or carved stone animal "fetish" as found in some Native American traditions. If you have something that can be used as a talisman or touchstone to owl, hold it in your receptive, or non-dominant, hand. If you are right-handed, then your left hand is considered your receptive hand. If you are left-handed, then your right is receptive. If you are ambidextrous, use any hand that feels right for you.

Relax your body and get into an alpha state. On the screen of your mind, call the image of an owl. What kind of owl do you see? How large or small is it? Perhaps it will be sitting on the image of a tree branch or in a nest. What color is it? What pattern is on the feathers? Does it make any noise, like the traditional "who" call that owls are known for?

Look into the owl's eyes and feel the owl looking back at you. Ask the owl to allow you to take its shape and form and fly free. Does the owl agree? Feel your awareness entering into this owl spirit. Become one with the owl. Feel your wings. Feel your claws as you perch in the nest or branch. Turn your head and be surprised at what it feels like to turn it around so much. How does your vision work? What is different about it? Get oriented in the owl spirit body.

Now, where do you want to fly? Do you want to travel in this world, or another? To what end? Have a destination in mind. You can travel over land to get from where you are to where you wish to be, letting your intention guide you. You can also use the Crystal Door to open gateways to other realms if that is your intention. Explore in the form of an owl.

When you are done, return to where you began. Thank the owl spirit for the journey, for allowing you to borrow its shape. Now separate yourself from the owl. Feel your arms become your arms, no longer wings. Feel your feet become your feet, no longer claws. Your skin is no longer covered with feathers. Your face is your own, no longer the feathery flower face with a beak. Become your familiar human self again.

See the owl before you once again. Thank it and say farewell. Erase the image of the owl from the screen of your mind. Give yourself Total Health Clearance and return your awareness back to the waking world. Remember what it was like to be an owl.

White Rabbit

The rabbit is an animal power that has long been associated with the Witch. Medieval Witches persecuted by the Church were said to take the form of a rabbit or hare and go to the Witch's Sabbat. Traditionally the rabbit is a symbol of cleverness, fertility, creativity, and the powers of the Moon. White rabbits are a sign of new beginnings. You can evoke the blessings of the white rabbit to bring new beginnings and get you out of past cycles that are no longer good for you. White rabbit is my primary totem.

Light a white candle. If you have any rabbit fur, put it in a white charm bag and hold it while doing this work. Rabbit hair traditionally speeds up any spell, so many Witches have it on hand as an ingredient for potions, charms, and incense. Speak this charm to evoke the blessings of the white rabbit familiar:

I will follow the white rabbit.
He has a new path leading me away from the past.
Bright new beginnings are to be.
White Rabbit, White Rabbit, White Rabbit
Three times three
White Rabbit, White Rabbit, White Rabbit
Blessed be!

Gaze at the white candle. Breathe deep. Listen to the sound of your breath as you draw in the air deeply and fully relax as you exhale. Attune yourself to the rhythm of your breath. Feel your heartbeat, like the patter of little feet, like the little feet of the rabbit moving in the forest. Feel yourself in the forest. You are walking a path. You can smell the rich green scent of the trees. You are walking along, enjoying this rejuvenating time in nature.

Up ahead on the path, you see a flash of white. You realize it is the white rabbit, running up ahead of you. You get close enough to catch a glimpse, and then the rabbit moves out of sight. You feel a sense of hope and joy just looking at the way it scampers on the path.

As you follow, you get a growing sense of urgency. The leaves rustle beneath your feet as you pick up your pace, trying to catch up with the rabbit. In the distance, you see a clearing, a grove in the forest. The rabbit is leading you there. As you catch up with the rabbit and enter the grove, you see in the center what you truly desire. What is it? What do you seek in your future? Is it a person? An object? A new home or job? An image of a new situation for yourself? The white rabbit has led you to your brighter future. Now it is your job to work towards this future and make the decisions to reach it with this newfound clarity.

Hold this scene clearly in your memory. Bring it into your heart and mind. Thank the white rabbit for this gift and let your sense of the grove and whatever is present within it fade away. Return your awareness to your body and gently open your eyes. Give yourself Total Health Clearance. Sometime within the next seven weeks, leave a little offering, such as some lettuce, outside for the white rabbit, and thank the spirit of the rabbit for showing you the way.

The Journey of the Horse

The horse is a teacher of power and swiftness. In the British mysteries, horses are the totem of British sovereignty in its oldest form, the horse goddess. Many goddesses have obvious and hidden horse associations. Most famous and most mysterious is the goddess Epona, with little lore surviving of her. Some associate the White Horse of Uffington with her, the chalk horse carved out of the hill. Epona is linked with Rhiannon, a Welsh goddess who is known to ride a beautiful horse and who is later treated like a horse as penance when accused of murdering her own child. Macha is the Irish goddess associated with both crows and horses. In one tale, she is forced to race like a horse while pregnant with twins because her husband boasted to the King of Ulster that his wife was faster than any of the king's horses. The king did not show her mercy and threatened the life of the husband. She won the race and gave birth to the twins on the finish line. Macha then cursed the men of Ulster to know the pain of birth in their moment of greatest need. The curse is fulfilled in the tale of the warrior CuCuhlain. Today, vestiges of horse worship and honoring can be found in the hobby horses of folk dances, where a horse head or horse skull is placed upon a pole and "ridden" around the land, often as a sign of winter. In Wales this practice is known as the *Mari Lywd,* and in England, the *Obby 'Osses,* where we get our term "hobby horse."

To me, horses are allies for strength and power. They teach compassion through strength in the same way that Rhiannon was able to carry on her back all who asked. Traditionally horseshoes were a part of the blacksmith's majick and were hung to bring protection and good luck to the home. I bead horseshoes with crystals and stones for protection, safe travel, and good fortune. They are to be hung over the door of your home and bring the power of the horse to your dwelling.

> To connect with the spirit of the horse, it is good to have an altar with the image of the horse before you. It can be a framed picture, a statue, or even a toy. Take some time to gaze at the image of the horse and think about the power and blessings of the horse. If you have access to any horsehair from any friends who raise horses, place it in a small bag of red, brown, or black, ideally matching the color of the hair, and hold it in your left hand. When you feel connected to the energy of the horse, enter into a meditative state.

> On the screen of your mind, call for the totem of the horse to show you your life. See a small point in the distance, perhaps against the background of a green field, moving towards you. With each moment, the image grows larger, revealing the form of a horse. The horse makes its way to you. What does it look like? Notice the shiny hair, the mane and tail. Is the horse wild and free, or is it wearing a saddle? What is the pattern of colors? How does the horse feel? Can you tell if it's male or female? When you look at the horse, you can sense its ability to communicate

telepathically with you. Ask its name and "hear" the answer in your mind. Take this time to get to know this horse spirit ally that has answered your call.

You have asked the horse to show you your life on its journey of power. The horse invites you to climb upon it and ride. Step through the screen of your mind and climb upon your new friend. Feel the mighty presence of the horse carrying you. How do you hold on? Feel the wind upon your face and hear the sound of the hooves as you pick up speed.

As you travel, you see the scenery moving along beside you begin to change. The power of the horse is giving you a journey of your life. You start by seeing your earliest memories, your child self and early growing up. What do you see? What do you remember?

As you continue the journey, you progressively see times that are older, and you might see things you don't consciously remember. Look at the journey of your life with your horse ally. What do you see? More importantly, what do you feel? Let it unfold before you, as if you are watching a movie.

Reflect on your own sovereignty, including both the times when you have ruled your own life and the times when you have felt you did not have control. What did you learn from these situations? As you ride, the horse spirit will speak in your mind and guide you to understand all that you see. Listen to this wise advice.

When done, you find that your horse friend has brought you back to where you began. Thank the spirit of the horse and climb down. Walk back through the screen of your mind, entering back to your sense of your body, and watch the horse ride out into the horizon. Clear the screen of your mind and give yourself Total

Health Clearance. When you are done, journal about the memories the horse has shown you on your life journey.

THE HEALING BEES

Bees are such a wonderful and forgotten animal power. Bees are associated with the ancient goddess of Minoan and Greek cultures, and Mycenaean tombs were shaped like beehives, showing a connection between bees and the ancestors. The Egyptians believed bees were made from the tears of Ra. Britain was known as the Island of Honey, and bees are associated with the mysteries of the Druids and bards. The Celts and the Norse were well-versed in the making of honey wine, or mead, and saw it as having divine properties.

Have you ever simply been with a bee? They are quite personable and gentle. If you are quiet and still, they connect well with humans. When the flowers are blooming next, seek out time in a garden or field. Seek out a place with bees and be with them. Watch them. Radiate a pink light of healing and love to them. They are great teachers of cooperation in community. I like to think of bees as nature's alchemists. They are masters of the art of transformation, turning flowers into honey, like lead into gold. Their honey is a powerful and potent medicine. In this meditation, seek out learning with the bees on all of these levels. They will be your teachers.

Enter into a meditative state and conjure the screen of your mind. In your mind's eye, call for the image and essence of a beautiful flower. The flower can be any type of flower you like, as long as it is beautiful and would attract bees to collect its pollen. Is it a flower you know from your majickal work? Is it a beautiful, exotic flower unknown to you? Gaze at the flower, taking note of all its shapes and colors, from the number of petals to the shape and feel of its pistil and stamens. Feel the energy, the vibration of the flower, and the blessing it conveys in its medicine and majick.

Once you have taken in all that you can from the experience of the flower, call out to the bees. Ask the spirit of the bee to come to you and to the flower, so you can learn its ways. Soon a worker bee comes to you and lands upon the flower. Climbing in, it begins its task of collecting pollen and nectar from the flower. Observe it all on levels. See the pollen collecting at the legs of the bee.

Feel yourself connect to the divine intelligence of the bee. The bee is part of a greater collective intelligence, just as we are all part of the divine mind. The hive acts like a smaller version of the divine mind for the bee, and the spirit of the bee is really the spirit of the collective intelligence of all bees. Through this single bee, the spirit of bee invites you to partake in its mysteries.

First, bees are excellent detectors of wellness. Just as they can scan the energy of flowers and trees, using a type of psychic ability and recognition of patterns, the spirit of the bee can detect wellness and help in your healing. The bee leaves the flower and gently begins buzzing over your body, starting at your head and moving down. Let it. As the bee buzzes, it is "reading" the energy of your body and looking for places of imbalance.

If the bee lands upon your body, you'll feel it "heat up" and begin to glow with a honey-gold light, filling that point of your body with its healing light, restoring balance to you. The bee might need to do this several more times to bring you into balance, and once it's done, you feel different, better than you did before.

The bee spirit invites you to experience life as a bee does, by shifting your shape to that of a bee. It can be startling at first. You might feel as if you are becoming smaller and smaller, and as you do, your body becomes rounder, growing wings. Feel them buzzing. Your arms and legs turn into bee legs, and you grow two more. Your stinger forms. Your antennae grow, and your eyes become the eyes of bees, seeing in a multitude of directions. You also realize you can "see" or feel the trails of light that connect all flowers and create patterns of flight for the bees. And in the back of your mind is the overarching presence of the hive, the distant hum, the song of the hive.

Your teacher bee begins to fly and beckons you to join it. Follow the bee. In the distance, growing closer, you see and hear and feel the presence of the hive. It has its own humming song. How do you perceive this hive? Pay attention to it not only visually, but by feeling its presence. Your guide makes its way to the entrance of the hive, and you follow.

The presence of your guide permits the guards at the entrance to treat you as a friend and allow you entrance. You enter a dark maze of hexagonal chambers and feel the presence of hundreds of other bees, all going about their work. None seem threatening or even particularly interested in you. Bees are coming and going, depositing pollen and nectar into various chambers. Your guide gives you a little tour, showing you the places where honey is made and the nursery where new bees are being hatched and nursed.

The constant hum of the hive's song gives you an understanding of the current work, season, and mood of the hive. There is a continual scent running through the hive, the scent of the queen.

Perhaps your guide will take you to have an audience with the queen bee herself. The presence of the queen is a blessing for any to experience.

Let your guide take you through the catacombs of the hive and experience the healing majick of the bee colony, whatever that might be for you.

When you are done, the guide takes you back out. You follow, still in your bee form, making your way back to the flower you first conjured, the place where you met this bee spirit. From this point, you are urged to take back your human shape.

Find yourself growing larger as your bee body takes the shape of a human body. Your antennae go away. Your head and eyes become your own head and eyes. Your abdomen becomes your own, with no stinger. Your legs become your legs, and your arms become your arms, and you no longer have an extra pair of insect legs. Wings shrink until they are no longer present, and you take the full human shape, leaving the bee shape behind. Reflect upon what you have experienced with the bee spirit and within the hive.

Thank your bee guide for this journey and teaching. Wipe away the flower and bee from the screen of your mind. Give yourself Total Health Clearance.

Work with the bees in your other healing majick. If you do psychic diagnosis health cases, you can call upon the bees to help determine where there is illness and imbalance in the body, asking them to restore balance with their golden honey light.

THE CHANGING SNAKE

Snake is a powerful majickal animal revered all around the world as an embodiment of the Goddess and the Earth. So many mythologies involve the snake. A popular image is the snake encircling the egg of creation, showing the role of serpentine energy as the creative impulse. The snake moves close to the Earth, upon its belly, in a waving motion that is not unlike the movement of the energy waves that encircle the planet. They are creatures of protection due to their constant movement and their awareness of what is around them. They can teach us to get close to the Earth, to be aware of our surroundings, and to move as needed.

Snakes are associated with the energy at the base of the spine, the *kundalini*, the divine feminine that is the consciousness of awakening, known as *Shakti* in the east. The snake is a symbol of psychic awareness, with the oracular priestesses of ancient Greece known as Pythonesses. Snakes follow their instinct, their intuition, which is the key to awakening our psychic ability. I have found that if you dream of snakes, they are warning you of enemies you didn't know anything about, and they will often show you in the dream how to best take actions to protect yourself.

Snakes are associated with the classical four elements of the magician. They are totems of the Goddess and have strong earth associations, helping us navigate physically in the world. Many snakes are native to swamps and marshlands, traveling quite easily in the water, and for some, water is their preferred habitat. Mythically, snakes are often associated with fire elementals, being described as serpentine and reptilian. The serpent of kundalini is sometimes called the fire snake. And while snakes don't have a lot of natural associations with air, some myths depict winged and feathered serpents, and science shows us the relationship between reptiles and birds is closer than most of us think. The image of the dragon combines many of these elements.

The big majick associated with snake is the ability to transform and change. Snakes are teachers of growth and embracing change. Snakes shed their own skins, letting go of the past and moving towards their new future. They can help us do that too when our old skin, our old identity, gets too tight and doesn't allow us to be something new. They teach us about the yearly cycle of life, death, and regeneration and help us embrace that change. In essence, they teach us to flow with the cycle of life that is already in each of us.

While we usually sit very still for meditation, when working with snake, it can be helpful to sway as you make a deeper connection to this animal spirit. So if you feel your body moving naturally, go with it. Don't try to fight it. Dance is an important part of many majickal traditions, and the power of snake will make you want to move like a snake, facilitating your connection to snake majick.

Take a moment to focus on the spirit of the snake. Invite the snake to you. Think about its qualities, the curves of its body and the flickering of its tongue. When you are ready, go into a meditative state. If you are counting down, you might find your pace of counting is in alignment with your serpentine swaying. Go with the flow of what is rising within you.

Gaze upon the screen of your mind and call forth the spirit of the snake. See the snake upon the screen. What color is it? What size? Do you know what kind of snake it is? Even if this type of snake is potentially deadly, this snake will not harm you. This snake is a teaching spirit here to help you. Can you hear it? Does it make a sound? Feel the presence of this powerful figure upon the screen of your mind.

When you're ready, reach out and hold the snake, just as you would in the Apple Meditation, except that this time you gather a snake. You will find that a lot of ancient creation stories have both the images of the fruit and the serpent, though Witches honor, rather than vilify, these as symbols of wisdom and life. Feel the snake in your hands. Gaze into its eyes. Hold it with love and tenderness. As the snake will care for you, you must care for the snake. You can feel it transmitting its wisdom to you directly, as if beaming an intuitive knowing to your mind just by looking at you.

Soon the snake will move of its own accord, slithering up your arm and then down your body. Starting at your feet, or near the base of your spine, it will begin to slowly rise up your body, perhaps entwining itself around you, coiling, or if it's a smaller snake, simply crawling up. As it rises up your body, you feel the snake energy enter you and empower you. The empowerment rises from the lower body, upward, until the snake is at the top of your head, at your crown, reminding you of the Egyptian crowns where a serpent is near the brow, a symbol of wisdom and power.

When the snake is at the top of your head, you have been permeated with the serpent's power. Your own inner powers and psychic ability have been unlocked. The serpent guides you to envision who you wish to be in the next step of your life. Who do you wish to be? What would that look like? Don't think just in physical terms; also imagine how it would feel. What would you know or sense in your new and empowered self?

Once you form a strong image of this new self, you'll feel as if your old self is like a skin, and it falls down around your feet as if you just slipped out of clothes that no longer fit. What remains is your newly refreshed and empowered self. How do you feel?

With this, the snake will slowly crawl back down to your hands. Say farewell and place the snake back upon the screen of your mind. Clear the screen and then give yourself Total Health Clearance as you return to your waking consciousness.

THE CROW OF PROTECTION

The crow is one of my favorite animals, bringing me so much majick and wisdom over the years. I named my second Salem shop Crow Haven Corner in their honor. Science is now confirming what Witches have always known, that these beautiful birds have deep intelligence and memory. The crow species is remarkable. They can live for thirty to fifty years. They have an intricate society, share information, and use tools. They recognize the faces of humans they come in contact with and tell their fellow crows which people to share space with and which people to avoid, not only issuing general warnings, but also relaying specific information about individual people and places.

Crows and ravens are associated with many of the primal goddesses and gods of the Celtic people, including the Morrigan and her associated goddesses Badb, Macha, and Nemain. Morrigan and Macha in particular are goddesses of justice, and you can ask the crows to help take a message to these goddesses. They sometimes perch on the buildings where I live. The sound of the crow immediately alerts me to pay attention to safety and to also watch out for people who would do harm.

Many times in my travels I have found crow feathers. Several years ago, I was traveling by car to Virginia for a Pagan festival. Halfway there we stayed overnight in a motel. In the morning, I was not sure why I had agreed to participate in the festival, and while waiting in the car to begin our journey again, I asked Macha if it was safe and correct for me to do this. All of a sudden, one single crow feather came spinning out of the sky and landed upright in the grass in front of our car. I knew Macha had heard me. I felt it was okay to proceed, that she, and the crow, were protecting me. The festival was inspiring, and no harm came.

Crows are teachers of sacred words and the power of our voice. They can learn to mimic us, speaking back like parrots. You can ask the crows for wisdom and advice, and in their "cawing" and response, hear a message that makes sense to you. If you listen to the voice of the crow, you might hear a "word" that is a word of majick power for you, one you can use in ritual to evoke the blessings of the crow. Many traditions teach that crows are the keepers of sacred law, majick, and wisdom.

I suggest people who want to work with crow should make a crow altar. You can use an image or effigy of the crow—a statue or framed picture. While I like to use three real crow feathers, technically it's illegal in the United States to own crow feathers, so any three black feathers will do. Light a black candle to the crow before you begin your meditation.

Close your eyes and see the dark goddess as the crow; see her spread her wings and soar into a blue sky. Hear her call *"caw, caw, caw"* and watch as she lands on a branch near you. Now you call to her in your mind, *"caw, caw,"* and in your mind, you hear her voice calling. Move quickly to her.

Gaze up into the tree. Now the crow looks down directly into your eyes, her black stare penetrating your soul, and at this moment, you become one with her. You begin to feel your shiny wings, and you are lifted into the sky, shapeshifting into the crow and merging with the crows in the tree before you.

Now you look down at the land below you. There is someone calling for the crow's help, your help.

You see a single black feather at someone's doorstep. It is the hiding place of a thief. What should you do to stop the thief at this moment? Three crows sail past you and land on the roof of this evil person's house.

They let you know it is not your job to punish or participate in stopping the thief. You are told the crow goddess Macha will decide their fate. You now know that all you have to do to catch the harmful person—a thief, a murderer, or worse—is to send a crow feather (or any black feather) to where they abide, and Macha will go there and mete out justice.

Your wings are heavy now, and you land where you began on the branch. You feel the feathers and the spirit of the crow leave your body, separating from you. Give yourself Total Health Clearance and come back into waking consciousness.

You will now fully understand what it means to harm none. Your judgement may not be sound. You must leave it to the wise crow goddess and her messengers.

You can become one with the crow anytime you feel the need to understand justice and sacred law better.

THE REALM OF THE LION

The lion is quite an amazing animal, with so many mythologies and stories associated with it. Majickally, lions are associated with the sign of Leo, ruled by the Sun. The lion-headed goddess Sekhmet was both a healer and a destroyer, a "lady of animals," and a beloved member of the Egyptian pantheon most associated with the power of the Sun god.

The lion archetype is frequently considered the "king of the jungle," the royalty of the animal world. Many European kings were associated with lions in name or through their emblems. The spirit of lion helps us be our own sovereign, our own ruler.

Like a good king, we must remain humble. The lion does not go around bragging about its abilities to other animals. Once we find self-esteem, it's easy to cross over into boasting, and lion helps us be on guard about being too egotistical. The purpose of the sign of Leo is to develop self-esteem without becoming too egotistical. Those who are truly regal are most often silent. They also help us understand our own kingdom, "our" people in our pride, and help us find our own treasure, meaning our own unique skills and resources, without taking too much unhealthy pride in them.

Envision yourself beneath the hot Sun as its power streams across a desert plain. You are walking through a land not unlike the Serengeti. Every step you take, you wade through the tall, dry grass. Feel the heat of the Sun above you, and the warmth coming off the sand beneath your feet.

Off in the distance is a large tree. It looks like it's the only tree in the world. Its branches spread out and cast a shadow, cooling the land beneath it. You seek a respite from the heat and move towards the tree and its cooling shadow. As you get closer, you see a very large lion resting beneath the tree.

His large fur collar frames his all-knowing stare. The wind carries your scent away from him, so the lion is not yet aware of your presence. You are tempted to walk closer until you hear a mighty roar come from his massive chest. You realize the wind has changed, and he has turned his head to spot you.

The lion's dark gold eyes draw you closer, making a laser-like connection with your own eyes. He peers into you, and you have become one.

You find yourself becoming the lion. You feel fur around your face, the beautiful mane. You feel the powerful muscles now gearing up to leap and run. You are the same as the lion, powerful and courageous, demanding of respect as you growl softly.

You feel the cool shadow of the tree. The wind is blocked by some of the dry grass moving across your body. You are waiting for night to fall so that you can roam the plains and allow your roar to echo into the surrounding hills, claiming your kingdom.

As you walk away from the tree, you shed your form and separate from the lion. Walking through the grasses becomes more difficult, and you realize you've taken your human form again, leaving the lion beneath the tree. You now stand far apart from this powerful lion spirit. He watches as you leave his domain. Give yourself Total Health Clearance and come back into waking consciousness.

Take the memory of your life as a lion with you into your human life. Take with you the courage, respect, and power of this being. Whenever you are confronted with trials, sense your eyes becoming gold like the lion's and kindling this power once again.

GROUNDHOG

The groundhog is a humble and often forgotten animal, especially by Witches who are seeking more famous and majestic animal allies. Yet we should remember the wisdom of the groundhog, as our modern Groundhog's Day customs are said to derive from older Imbolc and Candlemas celebrations.

Groundhogs dig their own homes, or burrows, and can help us with digging to get to anything in our own lives. I've found them to be the perfect ally to teach me the foundation of anything I'm questioning. They can bring you to the foundation of your home, your work, and your relationships, digging a tunnel that will show you what is really going at the root of it.

Digging signifies taking new steps and breaking new ground, but also the territory of our homes. Groundhogs don't like to let any other creature into their burrow, so in human terms, that means setting good boundaries and establishing some space and time for yourself.

Due to their long period of hibernation and their association with light and shadow on Groundhog's Day, these furry allies are about entering into dream trances and the mysteries of life, death, and rebirth. If you seek to understand the death and rebirth mysteries found in so many traditions, groundhog can be a great teacher. We speculate that those in the ancient mysteries would enter into dream incubation chambers as part of their healing rituals, and the groundhog has been naturally doing such majick every year. You can dream about your health, your happiness, or who you would like to be when you wake up and are "reborn."

When they awaken, they are hungry and seek out food. We say they are good at finding treasure, particularly lost treasure, but to the groundhog, treasure is what you can eat. If you are going to ask the groundhog spirit to help you find a specific treasure, you have to be specific when communicating with them. Holding an image of the treasure you value in your mind and projecting it to the groundhog you find in meditation can be helpful.

This meditation is a shapeshifting meditation, best done if you are lying down. You can do it inside or outside upon the ground. Relax your entire body and get into your meditative state by counting down into alpha.

Feel yourself surrounded by darkness, in the earth itself. In the darkness, feel your human shape shift and become fluid. Feel the shape you take become the shape of the groundhog, in the darkness. The darkness is soothing and nurturing. You are at rest, yet you are aware. Your sense of sound, of vibration, is much more acute, and you sense all sorts of things all around you in the earth.

In the darkness, you sense the most minute shifts of your environment, including shifts of light. You sense the light, the rising light, and follow your tunnel into the light, coming up into a grassy field. Walk through the grasses, sensing each blade of grass as you pass it with your body.

Follow the contours of the grassy field up the hill. Observe everything from the hill. Sense the beautiful grasses absorbing the sunlight as the Sun rises. You sense the temperature of the air and the presence of any wind.

Continue to explore the fields and hills as a groundhog. What do you sense? What do you see? How do other animals and insects appear to you?

Groundhogs have an innate sense of wisdom and knowing. What do you feel and know in this form of the groundhog? Let the wisdom of this animal come into you and express itself in your own consciousness. Affirm that you will remember.

Soon you sense the approaching storm. Without worry, you continue on your way, towards your home deep in the earth. You know your home cannot be flooded. It will stay warm and comfortable. The grasses and plants are your bedding and insulation. You go to your burrow before the waters hit. You hear the rain above, and the sound soothes you as you drift back into the darkness.

Intend to resume your own human shape and sense your form, your consciousness, flow as you feel your own body, your own hands and feet, arms and legs, head and body. Give yourself Total Health Clearance and come back into waking consciousness. You are now ready to count up from alpha and record your wisdom and impressions.

THE DARKNESS OF THE MOLE

Like the groundhog, the mole is also under-appreciated. While they share some commonality as creatures who dig, they are also very different. They teach us to trust what we feel, but not necessarily see, and help us improve our primal non-visual instincts on a psychic level. They cannot be deceived by what is before them because they can feel its essence and know the truth. With the help of mole, we learn how to feel something to know its true nature.

The mole is a mammal that dwells deep within the Earth. It has a small hind end and powerful forearms to help it move forward through the deep soil. With limited eyesight and a heightened sensitivity to touch and smell, the mole is in tune with the dark world below ground, connecting deeply to the Earth's minerals. Living on grubs and earthworms, the mole is a link in the chain of life. The mole helps feed the earth and soul to create new living nutrients. It relies on its heightened senses. It uses psychic touch to navigate its world below. Part of the blessings of the mole's majick is the ability to develop the psychic sense of touch. The mole has an incredibly gifted sense of touch, and it can lend its ability to us, to help develop and enhance our own. Let's draw on that energy to activate and empower your own psychic touch. This heightened awareness will aid you in self-healing and the healing of others, in your Witchcraft and the casting of your majick.

Moles are more in alignment with the darkness, with the unseen and invisible, having the sensitivity to be able to perceive what would be hidden and unknown to most people and animals. Like most digging animals, they can help us find hidden things, including our own hidden treasures. Mole spirit allies can help you see the unknown. Mole has helped me deal with those who are deceptive, especially those who steal. They can show you who is harming you and exactly what they are doing. You can call upon mole whenever you wish to go into places that are dark and hidden. If you ask, they will look and perceive what you can't see. You can merge with the mole and perceive things through their senses, through their own knowing of the dark.

Meditation with the spirit of mole can be disturbing for some people. Many Witches are very visually oriented. We train people to "see" with their psychic eye and to send energy in the form of visualized colors and light. The mole brings us into darkness, and that can be uncomfortable for some people. Like the mole, we need to open our own psychic senses beyond the visual to perceive things in the darkness.

Start by taking some rich soil from your garden or another area of land you have access to, or if necessary, any rich garden soil from a supply shop will do. Place the soil in a brown mojo bag with a moss agate stone. Moss agate helps us connect to the land and plants.

Find a comfortable place to lie down. This can be done indoors, or out in nature in a clean, safe place on the soil. Lie flat on your back with your palms facing down towards the Earth next to your sides. Place the mojo bag on your heart chakra. Count down into alpha breath—in through your nose and out through your mouth, descending deeper into alpha level.

As you feel your body relax, envision yourself connected to the dirt and earth. If you are comfortable envisioning yourself below ground, you may do so. Feel the cool earth all around. You hear sparkling noises from each and every mineral revealing itself to you and speaking to the minerals in your body, activating and enhancing and awakening your psychic sense and touch. Speak to your body now and say, *"I activate my electrolytes. My body is now clear and receptive to the Earth's healing. I am aware."*

Smell the rich soil as you breathe in and exhale. Speak, *"I am aware in this dark space. I see through the third eye and can feel the unseen world around me with my touch."* Raise your hands in front of you. Envision a landscape with grass and flowers. Run your hands along the tops of the blades of grass back and forth, feeling each blade as it bends, brushing against your fingers and the palms of your hands. Feel the blades of grass as they spring to a stand as you pass by each one. You now have reached a flower, taller than the grass. You run your hand up the stem, feeling all along the way. Feeling a leaf to the left of the stem, and a few more sporadically placed along the stem, you examine the flower. Feel the petals, soft like velvet, delicate. Feel the shape of the petals. Are they pointed? Are they round? Place your hands once again palm down by your sides, breathing in through your nose. Grasp a handful of dirt on either side with both hands, and at the same time, turn your hands over, palms up, and let the dirt run through your fingers.

Now you are ready to become the mole. Now you can see with your fingers, using them as you move forward through the dirt, using both hands pushing the dirt aside. Call the mole as a teaching spirit to you, to the screen of your mind. You will soon see the screen go very dark. How do you feel about the darkness? Why?

You are the mole. Bring both hands together in front of you, palms together, in prayer form. Speak, *"I am complete. My psychic sight is accurate and correct. Psychic touch is complete. The minerals within me are accurate and correct and aid me in my life."*

You become one with the mole. Rather than shifting your shape to become a mole, you merge with this mole before you, 'riding' its consciousness in the dark. As soon as you do, your awareness opens up. Despite the darkness, your sense of touch, smell, taste, and hearing are all sharpened. You have almost a radar sense of what is before you, and what is behind you, as you crawl in these tunnels.

The mole takes you to see something that has been hidden from you, something that would be in your highest good to be aware of. It could be something hidden and pleasurable, like a treasure, or something that has been used to deceive you, or something you have used to deceive yourself.

The mole brings you into a larger chamber in the darkness. You still don't see anything. But you listen. You feel. You become aware. What are you sensing? You might hear voices that identify who or what is hidden. You might get a "gut feeling" about what is going on in the darkness. Ask the mole to help make it clearer to you.

When you feel you have enough information, thank the mole. Raise your hands up to the sky and release the mole. The mole will then return you back to where you began. Leave the body of the mole, and feel your awareness take your own human form again, in your comfortable meditation position. Now you may start ascending upward. Take as much time as you need. You may randomly feel for the blades of grass on your hands. Breathe in through your nose and out through your mouth, until you see in your mind's eye a blue sky. Give yourself Total Health Clearance. You are now ready to count up from alpha.

You may remain at any stage of this meditation as long as you need. I want you to connect with your psychic ability and psychic touch to achieve this. Listen to your body. Pay attention to the energetic flow in the areas where you feel you need more time, as every person is unique to the experience. Don't be surprised if your eyes are more sensitive to light for a time. It will wear off soon enough.

Journal about your mole meditation and see if you can verify whatever hidden thing was demonstrated to you. Once you do, you'll know how powerful the wisdom of the mole is, and you can return to work with the mole when you need to uncover more hidden things.

SWIMMING WITH THE DOLPHIN

I had a client from New York City who went to swim with the dolphins in the Florida Keys two to three times a year. She would regularly come to Salem to have a reading with me. One year, she came back to share with me an amazing dolphin experience she had had. She had jumped off the boat, but there was one dolphin that wouldn't come near the group. She said out loud to the dolphin, "Do you have anything to say to Laurie Cabot?" It immediately came up to her. She felt the dolphin's message to me, through her, was "Come and see me." At that moment, the boat crew staff took a photo of her with the dolphin. She wrote "come and see me" on the back, but didn't say anything or show me the back of the photo. She just handed me the photo and asked me what I felt. I immediately thought the dolphin wanted me to come visit it. She told me to turn the photo over, and there was the same message. I can't swim very well, so I wasn't planning to go to the Florida Keys, but it did remind me of my own early childhood experiences with dolphin, and then I began to do more "swimming" with dolphin through meditations.

When I was seven years old, a dolphin saved my life. We were visiting friends of my parents in southern California, a very rich area, near an artist colony. The friends didn't have any children for me to play with, so the adults sent me out to the private beach to play by myself. I went out into the ocean, up to my ankles, then my knees, and soon up to my waist. The water was breaking not too far ahead of me.

Soon I saw the dolphin ahead of me, going back and forth. I went to step away from it, and it kept swimming up and down, almost as if it was standing up in the water. It was blocking me from going forward, going deeper, which is what I had been planning on doing. At first I thought it was showing off for me, so I took a step closer, getting the water up to my chest. I felt a wave of terror coming from the dolphin. It was sending a message to me telepathically. I got so terrified I turned around and got out of the water.

I told my parents and their friends what had happened, and their friend said there was a major riptide there, so perhaps the dolphin was saving me. I don't know if they believed that he was mentally communicating with me or not. Looking back on it, I believe he was trying to save my life, as I never would have survived the riptide and getting dragged out into the cove from the beach.

To experience the dolphin, I will go into alpha and "find" dolphins in the water willing to let me swim with them. They are amazing creatures, so agile and able to stop on a dime. When you are psychically in the body of the dolphin, your own physical body can lurch as you feel their sharp moves. I find them beautiful and amazing. Perhaps I have such an affinity for them and the freedom they embody because I am a Pisces.

To experience them yourself, enter into alpha state and hold the intention, "I will swim with the dolphins." Cast your mind over the land to the sea, seeking out a dolphin or group of dolphins in the water. Mentally ask the dolphins if you can join them, swimming together. If one dolphin agrees, imagine entering into the body of the dolphin, becoming one with it.

Ride with the dolphin, perceiving it as it travels through the waters and waves. Experience it diving and playing in the water. You might only experience the physical sensations, or you might become aware of the thoughts the dolphin is showing you, communing with you telepathically so that you may understand what it is feeling and thinking.

When you are done, thank the dolphin for this experience and hold the intention, "I will to return to myself." Feel yourself leaving the dolphin body and coming up out of the water. Say farewell and fly back to where you began, giving yourself Total Health Clearance and bringing yourself out of the alpha state.

THE DREAMING BEAR

The bear is a beloved totem and ally for us. While in life they are powerful and dangerous and shouldn't ever be approached in the wild, in meditation they are quite loving and comforting. Bears are associated with the wild goddesses of the ancient world, as well as figures such as King Arthur, as some consider his name to mean "bear king." Bears play a role in our stellar myths, with the constellations of Ursa Major and Ursa Minor, the Big Bear and Little Bear.

In tribal traditions, bear is the teacher of dreams because it spends so much time in its winter slumber. They teach us how to dream a new dream of our life, and how to take time out to rest and regenerate when we need to embrace stillness and darkness. While they can be fierce protectors with their powerful claws and teeth, more often than not, I find them as comforters, bringing me a sense of safety and concern for my well-being, like a mother bear caring for her cubs. In my visions, they cuddle and slumber with you, to make you comfortable and bring solace when life is difficult.

You can do this meditation lying down in bed, before going into sleep. It's powerful but gentle, and since the image of the bear is sleeping, it can lead quite well into our deeper dreams and leave us refreshed the next morning. Simply get ready for sleep and lie down in the bed.

Relax your body from head to toe and count yourself down to an alpha level. Then follow the visionary guide to the bear.

Enter the forest once again. The chill of winter is in the air. Perhaps there is some snow on the ground. Among the bare trees standing like skeletons without any leaves, the path into the woods is clear. Walk into the forest.

Each step brings you more clarity, more understanding. You know what you seek. You seek the bear, to sleep and dream with the bear, to find your own dreams and make them a reality. You move deeper into the woods, until you come upon the cave, the cavern that is the home to the bear.

You see the darkness of the bear cave before you. Gaze deeply into the darkness. Are you ready to seek your dream? If so, enter the darkness; surround yourself with the darkness. Using nothing but your intuition and your sense of touch, trail your hand along the cave wall and go into the earth.

Soon you will see the bear, illuminated by soft light coming through some cracks in the cave, slumbering deeply. The bear wakes up gently, and you feel welcomed by the bear. The bear spirit gazes upon you, looking deeply into your eyes, and invites you to look into its eyes, to see your dreams reflected in the eyes of the bear.

The bear invites you by movement and gesture to lie down with it, nuzzle up to it, and rest in the presence of its powerful body. The bear comforts and warms you from the cold air. The bear protects. In some ways, the bear is caring for you in midwinter, much like a bear cub. Bears will wake to give birth and care for their young amid hibernation. Contrary to popular myths, bears do not give birth asleep in hibernation. They wake, and this one wakes when sensing your presence, to help care for you. Will you be the bear cub for this time? Join the bear. Join the dream of the bear.

As you lie surrounded by the bear, snuggled and slumbering, you enter the bear's dream. The bear dreams of spring. You see the bear emerging from its cave and coming into the light. Behind the bear are small bear cubs running and playing. In some ways, rather than simply observing, you feel like you are one of the bear cubs running and playing. Follow the bear. The bear is digging for roots in the early spring. They are looking for nourishment. The roots help them return their energy levels and clear their lungs.

As the seasons progress, the bear seeks out other food and continues to play with the cubs. Bears can eat anything they want, and their day consists of the hunt for plants, berries, insects, fish, and other small animals. They might even wander into a human trash heap and feast on any leftovers they can find.

As the bear family moves through the seasons, the cubs get bigger. Summer comes. They climb trees. They play in the water. You are with them, climbing trees and splashing around in the cold streams and lakes. The bears might even seek out some honey and bees from natural or cultivated beehives. If you observe them seeking out the hives, be aware they eat bee larvae, not just the honey.

Fall comes, and they begin to slow down and shore up for the winter. They wander as the leaves begin to fall from the trees.

As the chill grows in the air, the bears prepare to retreat to their cave. Like a good cub, you join them, as cubs will stay a few years with the mother. Together you all return to the bear cave. As you do, nestling up again with the bear, you begin to dream. The bear "speaks" to you and asks to enter your dream. What do you dream? What do you desire to manifest? What would it be like if you did? Dream it first. The bear tells you that it will help you explore and manifest your dreams, for bear is the power of dreaming.

You hold the intention of your dream, and you slowly drift off to sleep.

When you awaken in your own bed the next morning, make sure you write down or record on a voice recorder whatever you remember of your dreams. The bear will give you keys in the dream for making them a reality.

THE GOD OF THE DEER TRIBE

The deer is one of the most powerful of the animal allies. Deer teaches us the power of our tribe, of our herd, and helps connect us to the people who are closest to us. The doe is the teacher of feminine strength and wisdom, manifesting as a horned goddess in wintertime, because only female reindeer keep their antlers in winter. The Celtic goddess Elen of the Ways is depicted as a reindeer goddess. The traditional male deer, the stag, is the teacher of male power. In traditional Celtic lore, the most majickal of the stags were those whose antlers contained seven tines, or prongs. The Druids and bards would seek the majick of the seven tines. I've found that you can ask the stag for the answer to a mystery, and you'll receive it, usually within seven days. The answer might not be direct, as it might come up in a casual conversation or in a book that crosses your path, but the answer comes.

Cernunnos is the Celtic horned god from the Gaulish times. Very little survives about him other than his name, though he's sometimes equated with the British folklore figure Herne. Many mistake him for a devil figure, but he's the Lord of the Forest. In the famous Gunderstrup Cauldron, he is sitting in a cross-legged pose amid a group of animals, holding a torc (a Celtic neck ring) in one hand and a horned serpent in the other. Many consider that to be a sign of his mastery within the natural world.

If you have access to any deer antler sheds (fallen horns from deer), place one before you along with a green candle. Light the candle and call the presence and power of the deer to you. Then relax your body and enter into an alpha state.

Breathe in and breathe out. Feel the animal power that is already a part of your body. As you breathe, get in touch with your animal nature. Feel the blood pulsing. Feel your heart beating. Feel your vital life force. Feel a cool breeze upon your skin. Gaze upon the screen of your mind; a forest begins to take shape. See the green leaves upon the trees, and the strong thick trunks climbing towards the heavens. There are so many trees that the sky is obscured, and you cannot tell if it is day or night. The smell of the decaying leaves and tree stumps is strong, but not unpleasant. All is as it should be in this forest world.

Step through the doorway of your mind and upon the forest path. The leaves crunch beneath your feet. You hear the creaking of the woods as trees gently sway in the wind. The presence of all sorts of small animals and insects surrounds you, but nothing intrudes upon your walk as you continue upon the path.

In the distance you see movement, a quick flash of brown and white. You see the hindquarters of some sort of deer. Is it a doe or a stag? You can't tell yet. Even though the animal is further ahead, evading you, it also seems to be leading you. Will you accept its invitation and follow?

You catch up with the deer, as it is lagging behind, allowing you to catch up. You are able to reach out and gently pat its hindquarters, and the full animal comes into view. How does it look to you? How does it feel? What kind of deer is your guide upon this path?

Your new deer friend, seeing you mean no harm, will lead you forward. Soon you are led to a herd of deer. They welcome you, and though they keep moving deeper into the forest, they allow you to follow. How many are in the herd? What do they look like? You notice some are old, and some are fawns. You see how they each take care of the other, old and young alike. And your guide is taking care of you.

Together with the herd, you make your way into a clearing in the forest. The sky is dark and filled with stars. A chill runs down your spine. There is power here.

At the furthest end of the clearing, there is a shadowy figure of a stag. You now know they are bringing you here to meet this stag. As you approach closer, the stag transforms into a stag-horned man. You see Cernunnos, the horned god of the Celts and master of the forest. He warmly welcomes you. His horns glisten in the starlight. Around his neck is a torc, a Celtic neck ring open in the front. Wrapped around his left arm is a ram-horned serpent. While human in appearance, he is as much stag as man. His presence is intense. He seems at one with the forest and all the creatures.

Speak with Cernunnos. Introduce yourself. Tell him that you came seeking the wisdom of the deer. What will he share with you? Listen deeply and truly. When you speak, speak from the heart. Cernunnos is particularly helpful in answering your questions around the mysteries and the unknown, and if he doesn't answer directly here and now, the answer will come in the form of a sign or message from another in seven days.

Cernunnos might show you the snake that he holds. Unlike traditional snakes, this creature has the horns of the ram, signifying its power and wisdom. Gaze into the snake's eyes, and as it flicks its tongue at you, a deep wisdom is transmitted into your soul.

When Cernunnos is done giving you this audience, your deer spirit will come and guide you on a path out of the forest. Follow the deer through the underbrush, with the fallen leaves and small scurrying creatures beneath. Come back to where you began. Say farewell to the deer, give yourself Total Health Clearance, and bring yourself to normal waking consciousness. Open your eyes and stare at the flame of the green candle. Let that candle burn in honor of the deer and Cernunnos, or snuff it and relight when you want to commune with Cernunnos again in the future.

Chapter 7: The Path of the Witch

Some visions are specific to those on the path of the Witch. They speak to our work in the world, manifesting our Witch heart, our Witch soul. They help us reach those deep inner places of majick where we find the power and strength within our blood. They guide the Witch through the world and this journey we call life.

THE MAJICK ROOM

The majick room is a powerful meditation to get to your own inner sacred space and make contact with your inner familiar, spirit guides, and power. Sometimes it's called an Inner Temple or a Soul Shrine, but whatever its name, it is simply the place within where you are empowered.

The meditation begins with a passive scene in nature. You can choose somewhere you have been and feel connected, such a beach, forest, nature trail, or mountain. Pick a place you really love or a place you would love to go but have never been. If you have not physically visited, it should be a place you are familiar with through photographs so that you know what to expect when you start the meditation. It must be a place in nature with no houses, wires, or any signs of civilization.

For this work, you will leave your body and walk into this scene in nature. It will not be on the screen of your mind, but a fully immersive vision within nature. You will experience it with all your senses, such as feeling the sunlight upon your face.

Light your favorite color candle and whatever incense empowers or relaxes you. Relax your body and close your eyes.

As you let go of all concerns from your daily life, you see yourself under a clear sky. As you bring your gaze downward, you see greenery all around. A soft breeze gently blows past you. The land is beneath you, and everything seems beautiful, perfect, and comforting. You are in the embrace of Mother Nature.

You see a small hill, and you go up that hill. At the top, you turn slowly around, taking in the view in all directions. You can feel the warmth of the Sun and smell the scent of many wildflowers in the fields. You are at the edge of the Earth and surrounded by beauty everywhere. Look at the whole of nature and start to see the curve of the Earth where the sky meets the planet.

In the distance, you see gray clouds forming at the horizon. The clouds are rolling in higher and higher. They roll over your head and blot out the sunlight. The breeze grows cooler. A mist of rain comes down on your face and your arms. As the clouds roll behind you, the rain grows stronger. Then, as quickly as they formed, the clouds roll away, and the Sun comes out. All the raindrops upon the landscape reflect the light of the Sun, and the Earth smells so good, refreshed and renewed.

As you look at the edge of the Earth once again, you see a rainbow forming. The end of the rainbow comes down upon you, bathing you in color and light all across the spectrum. Feel yourself immersed in the rainbow energy. Eventually, it dissipates.

In the distance you hear a rumbling. There is a roar growing, coming closer, like a train. Each moment it grows louder until the world begins to shake. Through the shaking, you gaze to your left, and a fissure opens up in the Earth. The rumbling subsides, and you gaze into the fissure, seeing layers of shale and bedrock as well as a few crystals revealed in the crack.

Look behind you, and there is a beautiful meadow of flowers, herbs, and grasses leading to a wooded area, a forest edge. There is something ominous about the forest, but you know that is where you have to go. From your vantage point, you see a path that leads into the forest, and you know this is the path to your majick room.

Come down the hill and walk through the meadow, moving towards the path that leads into the forest. The dark green leaves start to blot out the sunlight, with beams of light breaking through the forest canopy, illuminating the way. The trees feel ancient, moss and mushrooms growing on their bark.

The forest grows darker. The canopy folds in and shuts out the sunlight. It becomes difficult to see where you are going, so you have to rely on your intuition and sense of touch. A faery being may flit and float in the darkness, revealing her beautiful face to you. Her light illuminates the path and can guide you in the dark forest. You can now see the path back towards the meadow. The light begins to go through the forest once again.

As you walk, feeling the leaves beneath your feet, you know you are looking for the entrance to your majick room. It can take the form of an opening in the roots of a tree or at the base of a large stone. Find the gateway to your secret place. It belongs only to you.

Open the door and step down through the gateway. There will be steps beneath your feet, guiding you down. You'll soon find another door that will open for only you. Open the door and enter your majick room. It is a secret because only you know about it. If you share it with anyone, it is no longer a secret.

You find yourself in a large and spacious room, and you have the power to create anything you desire in this room. Start by creating a majickal throne, a special chair to sit and relax in this place of power. Using your inner vision, create a comfortable chair, and then continue to use your majick to create your room. Start by making two chairs next to you, one to your left and one to your right, and a small table.

You can create anything you want. Many Witches have a library filled with inner knowledge, though the library can take the shape of traditional bookcases, a modern computer or device, or even ancient record-keeping crystals. An altar with your tools would be a good start. Find or manifest your wand, chalice, blade, stone, and broom. You can even have a fireplace with a cauldron. A worktable or laboratory with herbs, oils, and bottles to make potions in the inner realm can be ideal.

Call to you the spirit of an animal familiar. What will appear for you? Your familiar can be the classic black cat, dog, or rabbit, or perhaps something more mythic, like a small dragon. This familiar will guide and teach you.

Make sure your majick room has a place for healing. What kind of tools do you want to use for healing? You can call people to your room and heal them distantly. Do you have a table where you can work your healing majick with someone? Is there a place you can go to receive healing and gather your own power?

Lastly there is a beautiful velvet curtain across the room. It covers a special gateway. This is the gateway of guidance, and through it, you can safely call your spirit guides and inner teachers.

Sit in your majick chair and open the curtain with your majick. Call to your highest and wisest guidance. Ask first for your female guide. Through the gateway behind the curtain, a female spirit ally walks into the room. Ask her to sit down next to you. Which chair does she take? Talk with her. What is her name? What does she have to share with you now? And then ask her to tell you of a time when she has helped you in the past. Have a conversation with her.

When you are done, open the curtain again and call on your highest and wisest guidance. Ask for your male guide to come through. When your male spirit guide arrives, ask him to sit down next to you and your female guide. Speak with him, asking his name and what work you are to do together. How he has helped you in the past?

Talk with both, as they are your first spirit guide team. Look at the details of these guides, from their facial expressions to their clothing. Try to learn everything you can about each of your guides. They will help you grow and evolve on the majickal path, being inner contacts in the world of majick.

When you feel this is done, thank them both and ask them to leave, but invite them to return when the time is right. Guide them through the gateway behind the curtain and close the curtain behind them.

While you look around your majick room, is there anything you'd like to change before you go? If so, envision the changes you wish.

As you grow, you'll make conscious changes to the room, and unconsciously, the room will evolve as you evolve. Ask your familiar spirit to take good care of this space for you while you are gone and remember to revisit it often.

Follow the way out, going through the inner door, up the steps, and out the gateway into nature. Mark the door with a secret sign or symbol that only you can see, to know this gateway is yours. Return to the space outside your majick room and become aware of the world. Feel yourself sitting, meditating in your chair, the physical world around you. Bring your awareness back to the present moment, give yourself Total Health Clearance, and when ready, open your eyes.

This longer vision shows us how we can control our environment in meditation and how we can extend that to better control our lives and environment outside of meditation. You are the cause of the weather changes and rainbow. You created the earthquake and opened the fissure. We manifest in our inner and outer reality.

You can return to your majick room anytime and find it to be a great education. When you return, your familiars might be doing their own work for you, making majick and conjuring things. You can relate to your familiars like you would pets and companions at home. My own black cat familiar is often on the mantle of my majick room, where he guides me. The crow in my room can talk like a parrot and answer questions I have. It tells me things I could not normally know. The familiars can keep your majick flowing and keep the room balanced. The changes in the room can reflect changes in you, and the changes you consciously make there can transform you and your life.

Here are some ideas to explore when you return on your own:

Majick Circle—You can paint a majick circle on the floor where you can do formal ritual in the meditation, just as you would in the physical world. Your circle can have an altar with all the tools you have, plus any tool you wish to have.

Healing—Your healing place is almost like a shower, where healing light will rain down upon you from above. Like the Egyptian Sun meditation in **Chapter Four**, the ball of light above you can separate into different healing colors. Simply stand under the ball and asked to be healed. The proper healing color will be sent to you. When I do this meditation, I get really warm as I fill with the light. Electric blue has been my most vivid and powerful healing color, but we will each have our own power color, and that color can change depending on what is going on with us.

Apothecary—Your majick room can be well-stocked with herbs and oils to make potions. When I go to my apothecary work bench, I ask for whatever herbs I need for a specific intention. The herbs come forward themselves to reveal their use. If an herb comes forward that I am unfamiliar with, the name might pop into my head when I hold the jar in meditation. Later I will learn it was a real herb, perhaps with a different folk name I wasn't familiar with. You can make the herbal mixture in the majick room and have its majick work, and you can also retrieve formulas from this place and use them to create physical potions to share with others.

Library—Your study or library is filled with the information you need. Go to the library and ask, "What should I know?" and amazing things can appear in the books. You can even have the experience of automatic writing with the pens and papers in the library. Asking "should" is always better than asking for what I "want" to know, as wants can conjure illusions. The library can reveal lost books. I've found some written by monks I believe were really Witches. I couldn't always read the writing clearly, but the very presence of the book triggered changes in me for the better.

Time Travel Machine—I envision a time machine reminiscent of something out of a steampunk or H.G. Wells novel, filled with levers and dials allowing me to choose a specific time, date, and year. You can program the machine to take you to other times and places. You travel through a bright light and when you "land," the machine is invisible and only you can see it, though people from that time and place can see you once you leave it. I find traveling through my time machine to be better than Tarot or a crystal ball to look at both the future and past.

Crystals—On your desk you can create a variety of crystals. Those crystals can have the same properties as natural crystals, based upon their color and type, but they are also used to manifest things in your life, for they can be charged with intention. Some crystals can open doors in the room, acting as a key. Each crystal will have its own unique purpose waiting for you to create or discover.

THE WITCH'S WALK

Walking can be a meditative action. The rhythm and repetition of our steps is a powerful technique to enter into a light alpha state. We think deeply and become inspired on long walks. I love walking around Salem on a crisp fall day, my black cloak billowing in the wind. And I've loved my long walks in the woods looking for items to use when crafting my potions and tools or for when I make items to share majick in my shops.

Decide to meditate on the Witch's Walk. Plan on where you wish to go, choosing a route with a beginning, middle, and end so that you don't get lost. You can do this in a quiet town, in the woods, or on the shore. You can trace a loop returning to where you started. Just make sure the area is not so busy that you have to worry too much about cars, pedestrians, and your own safety. Though you should always be mindful of your own safety when walking alone, you do want to have the freedom to contemplate deeply as you walk.

The intention of the Witch's Walk is simple. We often think of the Goddess, and ourselves, as maiden, mother, and crone, the triple goddess. We can also think of the maiden as the warrior and huntress, the mother as the queen, and the crone as the wise woman. Male Witches might think of the triple form as youth, father, and sage. The youth can also be the young warrior and the father the king. The sage is the magician or trickster as well. We use these images to look at the journey of life, at our own path, and reflect on what we have done and who we have become.

As you walk, you can feel as if you are walking with one of the three images and allies, each in their turn. In your mind, speak to them and let them speak back to you, offering advice, perspective, and wisdom.

For the first third of your walk, envision you are walking with the maiden or youth. Reflect on your early life. What did you do? Whom did you know? What would do again? What would you do differently knowing what you know now?

For the second third of your walk, feel the maiden or youth step back to the mother and father, the queen or the king. Walk with these sacred sovereigns. Talk about midlife and the work you have done in the world. Speak of your own sovereignty and strength in the life you have built.

For the last third of your journey, walk with the elders, the crone and the sage. What wisdom do they have to offer to you? Listen with an open heart and mind.

Return to where you began and feel the presence of the three within you. Know that all three are with you whenever you walk, as all three are with you all the time. Learn to draw upon their strength and wisdom, for they are aspects of your own majickal self.

LIQUID MOONLIGHT

This simple meditation can be done as a ritual, but when done as a meditation, it can deepen the experience and also teach us that we can still do majick even when we don't have our tools readily available. This is one of the simplest yet most profound of the Witch's rites, drawing down the Moon into the chalice and drinking it in.

Count yourself down into an alpha state. On the screen of your mind, envision a perfect silver chalice filled with the purest spring water from deep in the Earth. Next to it is a perfect majickal blade, a double-edged knife of steel or crystal. With one hand, reach out and take the chalice. With the other, reach out to take the blade.

Gaze upward and see the full Moon above you in the night sky. Contemplate the beauty of the night, of the Moon and sky. Contemplate the majesty of the Goddess.

Gaze into the still waters of the cup. Catch the image of the Moon in the water, shining like a silver mirror. Slowly see your own face in the light of the reflected Moon upon the water. Gaze deeply at your reflection. Look into your own eyes, into your own soul.

Envision thrusting your ritual blade, your athame, into the liquid, shattering the Moon and yourself into shards of crystal. The crystals dissolve and mingle with the water, becoming one with the water, and you drink the water, draining the chalice dry. You have become one with the water, with the Moon, and with your very soul. You are in union with the love and power of the Moon goddess, and she dwells within you.

Count yourself up from alpha, give yourself Total Health Clearance, and feel the Moon goddess' power within you.

BALANCE OF THE MOON AND SUN

This meditation appeared in my book, *The Witch in Every Woman*, in a story called "The Queen's Embrace." I wrote about a woman meeting a queen upon a gaming board in the dark woods under the full Moon. The queen gives her the Moon and the Sun to hold, and upon daybreak, leaves her in perfect balance upon the board, the Game of Life. Little did I realize that several years later, I would be in Stonehenge, casting circle, and at one perfect moment as the Sun set and the Moon rose, I stood with one in each hand and was like the woman on the game board, in perfect balance, as we continued with the majick of our circle. We can create that same balance within us, anytime we need it, by following the pattern of balance, like the scales, with the Sun and Moon.

Enter into an alpha state and envision yourself walking along a forest path at twilight. Go deeper into the forest, smelling the earthen scent of the fallen leaves and hearing the crunch of the twigs breaking beneath your feet. Small nocturnal animals, waking up for the evening, scurry around you.

The path rises up a hill, and at the top, you come upon a large clearing with an ancient stone circle in the center of it. Stand in the center of the circle, taking a close look at the ancient and weathered stones. Marks and lines are carved upon them, peeking out of the lichen.

As you center yourself in this place of majickal power, you see the Sun setting to the west and the Moon rising to the east. You reach out and take the Moon in your right hand, facing the north. Traditionally the right hand is masculine, projective, in most people, and the Moon is the balance to this power. You hear the song of the Moon when you reach out and touch it, holding this silver sphere of light in your hand. What does it sound like?

You continue reaching out to the Sun in the west with your left hand. As you hold the golden ball of light that is the Sun, you hear the song of the Sun. What does it sound like? Your left hand is receptive, so the Sun's projective power is balanced. Likewise, the east is about rising, balanced with the receptive power of the Moon, and the west is receptive, balanced by the projective power of the Sun.

Stand in the center, in perfect balance between the Moon and Sun, the east and west. Feel yourself like the scales of justice, like Ma'at, the Egyptian goddess of balance, or Themis of the Greeks. You are the fulcrum itself, balancing all polarity. You become an embodiment of the Hermetic Principle of Polarity, representing the true balance between. Hold this vision of balance as long as you can. Hold it until the stars turn, and you realize you must "let go" of the Sun and Moon so they can continue their journey, but know that they have left you balanced.

Follow the path down the hill, back the way you came through the dark forest. Return to where you began and find yourself returning to your body awareness. Return from alpha when you are ready, giving yourself Total Health Clearance and returning refreshed and rebalanced.

THE VISION OF THE WISHING CANDLE

You don't always need a candle to do candle majick. Candles work through the power of light, and we know that our mind's eye also conveys the majickal power of light for our intentions. Think of an intention you wish to manifest through candle majick. Get clear on the intention, on exactly what you wish to happen. What color best corresponds to it? When you do candle majick, what kind of candle do you like? Do you prefer taper candles? Larger pillars? Small birthday candles? Any can be used for this meditation. Do you have a preference for candleholders? I prefer old-fashioned brass candleholders as they conduct majick the best.

When you are ready, get into alpha by counting yourself down. Once at alpha level, conjure the perfect color and shape candle to match your intention, including the right candleholder for you. Next to it, envision a majick wand. The wand might be one you already possess, or it could be some grand vision of your idealized wand. Reach out and take the candle in one hand and the wand in the other.

As if the tip of the wand can write or carve, use it to write your name down one side of the candle along with a simple summary of your wish, such as "love" or "healing," upon the other side of the candle. When this is done, focus upon your intention and point your wand at the flame, igniting the wick of the candle.

Place the candle back upon the screen of your mind, and as you do, see the intention symbolically or literally manifesting in the space around the candle. The candle will majickally "float" there in the space before you. For example, you could see cash or coins of gold growing around the candle for a money spell. Hold the vision for as long as you can, and the candle will continue to burn, faster than a physical candle. Let the candle burn until it is out, and soon your wish will come true.

Count yourself out of alpha, giving yourself Total Health Clearance, and return to waking consciousness, confident your majick is at work.

THE ANCESTORS

The ancestors are those who have gone before us. They are the beloved ones of our family, as well as the mighty ones who have preceded us on the path of the Witch. They come forward and want to help us on our path and in our majick. Sometimes we want to connect with a specific loved one, but that ancestor won't come forward. Some need peace and rest after death, and must take time to really recognize and review what happened in life before they are ready to come back and visit their family as an ancestor. Be patient and don't take it personally. The key to ancestral work is repetition and perseverance.

While some unknown ancestors can pop up from time to time, you ideally should know them before they answer you. They can appear as a group, but it is best to meet the ancestors one by one, spending special time with each.

Start by building an ancestor altar on a curio shelf. You don't have to use a candle, particularly as you don't want to burn the inside of the shelves, but start with pictures of your ancestors if you have them, and any objects that would connect you, such as an article of clothing, glasses, or their favorite perfume or cologne. If they had another favorite scent you can duplicate, then use that instead. Pick a specific time to do this work and go to this shrine every day at the same time. Call to your ancestors and talk to them. Invite them; do not command. Speak about how much you miss them and want to know them. If the grief is fresh, tell them of your sadness, but also tell them that you know they are alive in the otherworld and that you welcome them to visit you. Do this every day until you have contact.

Contact might not be what you expect. When you ask a question of the person on the other side, the answer might sound like it is in your own inner voice, that you are making up the answer. Keep a journal, and if you get an answer to your question, even if you think you are making it up, write it down. The more you keep the journal, the more you'll realize your answers are from the ancestors, as information will be revealed that you couldn't have consciously known. But it can take some time to know this is real. Eventually you might hear their voices or see them in your mind's eye or catch the outline of them in the room. They dwell within us, within our blood, so of course the answer will sound like it comes from us, as they are reaching through us, through our common DNA, to speak. Spirits use what is in us already to communicate, but it doesn't mean the contact is any less real or valid.

When you are sitting with someone to read their ancestors, say silently, *"I will allow a person from the otherworld to come forward if they have something to say to this person in front of me."* Before I go into the message, I talk to the spirits to tell them to come through for something important, not just to chit chat! I can't deal with just the chit chat. Otherwise the needed message can be lost in the chatter. Then I wait until I hear, see, or feel in my mind's eye. Sometimes I know how it is connected to in the person before me, and sometimes I don't know and just have to announce it, passing the message along. At times it can be awkward, such as when the spirit of the departed husband tells his newly married wife, "You married that jackass, and he's no good." I didn't know she had gotten remarried, or even that she was widowed, so you have to be willing to bring the message through, no matter how strange for you.

THE MYSTERIOUS PLANET VULCAN

The planet Vulcan is a mysterious planet theorized by esoteric astrologers as the secret ruler of Taurus. While not accepted by mainstream science, esotericists have been working with the power of Vulcan for a long time. I was originally told of Vulcan by the Rosicrucian master, Master Thomas, of the Brighton Massachusetts lodge, and he taught me this powerful meditation to experience the energy of Vulcan.

Vulcan always reminds me of the ancient Druid priests and priestesses who were said to wear large collar necklaces with many colored jewels to enhance their majick. Today, we know the crystal can be activated by pressure, such as the piezoelectric effect of quartz. Crystallography became a science in 1783, yet the ancients seemed to understand something that took us a long time to discover. And perhaps the effects of Vulcan help those sensitive to its energy understand.

Vulcan is considered a planet too close to the Sun to be detected. The extreme heat of the Sun has turned all of Vulcan's minerals into pure brilliant gems, like the crystal caves of the Naica Mine of the Mexican state of Chihuahua.

The meditation of Master Thomas is to be done on Sunday, as the Sun rises, for the best results.

> Face east before dawn. Sit quietly and count into alpha, staying as still as possible, and do not open your eyes. Do not move your hands or feet. State in your mind, *"I will ready myself to travel to Vulcan."*

> First prepare for the heat of the Sun. See yourself covered completely with thirteen inches of twenty-four-karat gold, covering every inch of your body like a suit of armor. Every part of your body must be covered by gold.

On Sunday as the Sun rises, you will travel on the first ray of sunlight as it strikes the Earth. You are hit by the first ray, and you are instantly transported to the face of Vulcan. You are standing on a mammoth green jewel as you land. It extends for miles as you look down upon the green gem. It is so clear you can see miles down into the planet from the surface. While on this green gem, ask, "Is there is anything I should know?" Stop and listen, allowing the knowledge to come. If information does come, state to yourself, "I shall remember all I have heard and seen."

Step off the green crystal to another gem, possibly a red ruby or bright white diamond. As you touch each gem, ask each, "Is there anything I should know?" and allow each to answer you. Continue as long as you are comfortable, exploring different gems and crystals.

With your gold heat shield, you might be feeling very hot. If the heat is overwhelming for you, it is time to leave Vulcan and return home.

Beams of colored light shine towards the Sun from Vulcan, and rays of light travel from the Sun and touch the Earth. Travel from whatever color gem you are standing upon towards the Sun's rays, upon that color beam of light. Let the colored ray of Vulcan carry you to the Sun, and then the Sun's rays will return you back to the Earth.

You find yourself seated where you began, shedding your gold shield all around you. The pieces of gold disappear into the Earth. Thank the universe for the knowledge you have received. When you are ready, give yourself Total Health Clearance and count up from alpha.

Write down all you remember from each jewel. Add this knowledge to what you already know about colors and crystals associated with the planets. In majick, Vulcan is the jeweler of the gods and grants power and wisdom to your spells.

THE TWIN OF SPARTA

Once, in deep meditation, I was transported to another planet. I had traveled beyond the Sun, and in fact to the opposite side of the Sun. There I found a new planet, much like Earth. As I landed down and touched the soil, I realized this planet is exactly like Earth with one exception—no humans inhabit Sparta, only animals. Many of the animals are ones we thought extinct; others do not exist in our physical world, only in the realm of fantasy. They are reality on Sparta, which is the pristine twin of the Earth.

Sit quietly and count into alpha, relaxing deeply into your body. State in your mind, *"I will ready myself to travel to Sparta."*

Feel yourself rise up from your body and into the sky above you. Float through the sky and past the clouds. Float into the orbit of the Moon and beyond, into the solar system. Follow the orbit of the earth around the Sun, moving between the orbits of Venus and Mars. Keep going until you move past the Sun and lose sight of the Earth from the arc of the orbit. Soon you will see another Earth, the twin of Earth, Sparta.

You descend through the orbit, and you can't tell if Sparta has a Moon or not. You pass through the clouds and into the pristine air. As you land, you come into a field of waving grasses. Walk around and orient yourself. You realize the entire planet looks pristine, like a nature preserve or park, but there is no "civilization" anywhere. Everywhere you look is green. The sky is blue and clear. There is no pollution. The rivers are clean and clear. The breeze is warm and soft upon your skin. Wildflowers fill the field. And you see a lush green forest not far in the distance.

Before you stand a unicorn mother and her baby. Their coats are extremely white, and the baby's horn has not fully grown. Their eyes greet you with acceptance. You are welcomed. You belong. You realize that you are experiencing what the Earth was like before humans, in the ancient mythic age where all is possible. It enlivens your Witch soul. As the unicorns go about their business, you explore, looking for animals and plants. You encounter waterfalls and bubbling brooks filled with fish. All welcome you without fear. They don't know fear without humans. Everything is a paradise.

Feel your body cleansing itself of all illness and pollution. It cannot exist here, as if your body is undergoing a primal 'reset' to its system. Your mind, body, and spirit are balanced and in harmony. You feel yourself in peace and balance.

Prepare to travel back to Earth, remembering the gifts the planet Sparta has given you. Return the way you came, rising up from Sparta, through the clouds, following the arc back around the orbit of the Earth and its twin until you see your familiar planet waiting you. Descend again past the Moon, into the atmosphere and through the clouds, until you return to where you started.

You find yourself seated where you began. When you are ready, give yourself Total Health Clearance and count up from alpha.

Write down your experience and track how your health changes for the better from this point forward. If you need a reset again, you can always return to Sparta, and with each visit, commune deeper with the land, animals, and consciousness of the entire planet. She has much to share with you about what could be on the Earth.

Root Race Meditation

In 1975, I was in the company of several Witches one evening, and we were discussing the origin of human life and all the possibilities. I wanted to go back to learn how human beings came to be on Earth, to see the beginnings of our race via time travel. The group counted me down into a very deep trance and recorded my vision of an ancient land more suited for what I considered mythology than anthropology.

I saw a different landscape with advanced civilizations upon island nations connected by stone causeways. There was a civilization stretching from Egypt and Greece all the way to the Bimini Islands. There I was shown a story of various entities, seemingly alien gods, created races of brightly colored people. There were five main temple pyramids upon five islands, each with its own god. I was shown that each god came from a different star system, and Earth was a collaborative project. The five solar systems are represented in the five points of the pentagram.

Bright red humans were made in the image of the goddess Isis. Blue people were made by a figure akin to Hermes. The remaining three races were jet black, peach or orange, and a lime green bordering on yellow. The gods associated with these remaining three were not clear to me.

The temples were also schools where the newly engineered, brightly colored humans were shown large sheets of metals etched with strange writing. The writing was their programming, giving them everything they needed to survive. The gods then paired different couples of differing colors and placed them in various areas of the world to start the human race. The various combinations created the seeds for the races and tribes we know today, as the colors became the more "muted" skin tones we are familiar with now.

After following the causeway, I saw a small pyramid in front of me. Next to me was a man with blue skin. He brought me into a large classroom space filled with humanoid beings. The blue man said he was the teacher. The beings were cloned in his likeness, male and female. He stood at the front of the room and before him were metal tablets inscribed with strange symbols. He raised a crystal, and all the students came to attention. He then raised one metal tablet at a time for the blue people to see. He pointed the crystal at the class. There were seven tablets in all. Everything they needed was on those seven tablets.

Soon the scene shifted, and I was flying, holding hands with another being with red skin. We were flying down the causeway to another pyramid. In this pyramid, the same thing happened, only with red-skinned beings. Seven tablets were shown, each marked with strange writing. The process repeated three more times with jet black, peach, and lime-green people learning from seven tablets. The tablets were various forms of copper and silver scrolls and gold plaques, yet the writing could change on them, and each temple had seven.

I was then told there are five root races from five different solar systems. Each were there for a great experiment, trading goods and resources. Upon their "belt" was a buckle with a pentacle, symbolizing the five races' agreement to this experiment. Each of the five decided to place representatives of their species here upon the Earth two by two, to explore their genetic potential in a new environment and to see what happened as Earth evolved. While this defies conventional science on every level, I was told it began three hundred million years ago.

The pyramids around the world were way stations for the teachers of the five races. I was shown a vision of where these technicians around the earth were, and then images and names of where they are from. I remembered Pleiades, Sirius, and Orion, and two that were not clear to me. The technicians left earth, I was told, and those technicians are still alive and now live on their home planets.

After a few million years, the experiment was not going so well, so they got rid of all of it through a Great Flood. The experiment was stopped a second time, through a great fire. We currently live in the age of the third experiment. They have not yet decided if the experiment is to be ended.

I know this sounds fantastic. I was as surprised as you, and often hesitated to share this in my Witchcraft classes. The idea of humans descending from aliens seems strange to me, but also there was something very true to it. At the time I was not familiar with the ancient astronaut theory, or the work of the author Erich von Däniken and his book *Chariots of the Gods*. I was familiar with the Barney and Betty Hill alien abduction story from New Hampshire, but had no idea about ancient aliens. Soon I would be introduced to these ideas, and they would bring greater clarity to my vision.

The results of it helped me understand some childhood experiences. When I was little and scolded by my parents for doing something wrong, I would run outside crying and look up into the sky. I'd lift my arms and say, "I want to go home." And I expected someone from above to get me. At age three, it was quite a concern for my parents. It became something in me that I have always known we come from the stars. I felt certain my childhood cry was a genetic memory of some deep knowledge.

Yet what do we do in an age where we know scientifically that race is simply the physical and cultural adaptation to various regions? There are no races. We are all of the human race. The Theosophical idea of Root Races came from a prejudiced time and age, looking at some of the modern ethnic groups as superior in some way to others. We don't believe that today. So what do we do with information that guides us to such a wild concept of race, both human and alien?

I think the vivid color imagery speaks more to a majickal reality than a genetic, ethnic, or regional one. The bright colors of my vision speak of auras, energy, and otherworldly awareness. Exploring your root race explores the energy line from which your soul first incarnated here upon the Earth.

I now share it in our Witchcraft classes, precisely because it is a mind-expanding idea, and the meditation to go with it helps break down our expectations and assumptions. It helps us understand what the ancients knew, that our race is from the stars, and that our ultimate mystery is found in the cosmos.

Get into a comfortable position for meditation and count yourself down into a deep state of alpha. Hold the intention to visit the origin of humanity, and the root race of your soul. Draw in white light a flaming pentagram upon the floor, as an anchor to return to this place and time, and then rise up. Rise up from this place through the ceiling of the building you are in, into the sky and clouds, until you are high above the Earth, looking down. Look down, and let the Earth turn backwards in time, back to the dawn of humanity.

Descend downward and fly over the ocean, looking down upon it. In the Atlantic Ocean, you will see several large islands, with pyramids of varying shapes and sizes. The islands are connected by magnificent bridges. In fact, from a distance, the islands almost appear to be a path of gigantic stepping stones leading towards a continent of unfamiliar shape.

You notice there are five larger main islands, with a large pyramid complex upon each. Which of the five islands calls to your soul? Project yourself towards it, entering the temple. There within the temple structure, upon a large throne, is an alien god. Before the god are humanoid figures, lined up as if in a classroom or school. What color are the figures? Are they red, blue, black, lime green, or peach? Which of the figures calls to your soul? Join with this figure and experience the events through the eyes of this ancestor.

You are shown a large sheet of metal with esoteric writing upon it. One slab of metal rises up, and you absorb and process the information instantly. It is then taken down, and another slab is raised. Perhaps the Emerald Tablet of Thoth originated here, along with other mysterious tablets of majick and teaching. The god upon the throne oversaw this process of education.

As you read this information, you are told everything you need to know. You understand these five beings come from five solar systems, and you were made in the likeness of the god before you. You understand that one group came from the Pleiades, but their origin was from beyond the Pleiades where they first intermingled. They chose Earth as a remote planet so no one would interfere with their experiment. They did not want aliens outside of their pact to interfere with the development of humanity. You see an image of the pentagram, and see how the five join together in unity, and why the pentagram is such a powerful symbol for us today.

Once this information is within you, the gods begin to pair up with others from the different temples or perhaps from the same temple. Who are you paired up with? From which root race do they come? The gods then begin populating the world with differently matched couples. Feel them take you across the world. Where do they place you? You are not afraid, as you realize you have all the knowledge necessary to not only survive, but to thrive in your new environment.

Find your awareness slipping out of this body and observing the evolution of the entire world. See the development of the people, the mingling of the different root races creating people closer to what we know today. Each of the root races had specialized knowledge including topics of language, survival, food, shelter, clothing, mechanics, masonry, music, culture, and art. Many focused their efforts on technological achievements while others focused upon more artistic pursuits. Some were masters of majick.

See the ancient aliens destroy some of their temple bases, including the bridge system. They leave the colonies, and the new humans imitate the old temples through the pyramid system across the world. Some created great buildings and temples, and others did not.

Rise up and return to the heavens. Look at the Earth below. Allow it to turn and turn until you return to your current time. Let the white light pentacle guide you back down to the Earth, back down to where you began, reuniting your awareness with your body. Give yourself Total Health Clearance as you count back up from alpha.

THE CRYSTAL WHEEL MEDITATION

In 1975 the Black Doves of Isis coven of the Cabot Tradition psychically constructed the Crystal Wheel that exists etherically over Salem, Massachusetts. To those viewing it psychically, it looks like a ring of large quartz crystals surrounding the border of Salem. We created it as a majickal conduit for information, protection, and healing, and we encourage people to go there to seek solace and help for the highest good of all involved. Many spiritual traditions and lodges will offer their services and take petitions for others in need. Through the Crystal Wheel, we do the same, and having it exist on the psychic planes means it is available to anyone, anytime, through simple meditation. We've had many miraculous reports of the wheel's majick from people all over the world.

Every week, Cabot Witches across the world go there on Thursday at 10 p.m. Eastern, adjusted for local time zones, to recharge and be a conduit for healing and answers to those who seek. The circle lasts about an hour, and each week we focus on a specific color to change the wheel and narrow our intentions, though anyone can meditate upon it through meditation at any time. Sometimes people have no conscious knowledge of the chosen color, but see it when they visit psychically, showing us all how effective the work with the wheel is. Priestesses and priests in our community collect and gather lists, often through social media. We place all the names and intentions into a special cauldron attuned to the crystal wheel before we begin on Thursdays. Others join us in meditation to offer help, or to seek help, even if they are not on the list. Some hold a crystal of the chosen color or a simple quartz point in their left hand when doing the work, envisioning it as one of the many in the great ring of crystals. While we as individuals don't solve any problems or heal anyone, we become conduits for the energy to flow to others from the universal mind through the Crystal Wheel.

To experience the Crystal Wheel Meditation, enter into alpha using the Crystal Countdown method. Envision yourself as your double, like stepping out of your physical body and into a spiritual body that carries your perceptions and awareness. You leave your physical body behind, ideally in your Protection Shield (as explained in **Chapter Three**) and feel yourself rising up, going at least seven hundred feet above the Earth. You go into the sky above you and feel a magnetic pull towards Salem, Massachusetts. You are moving as fast as you can think, and no matter the physical distance, you are soon there.

You see before you an immense Crystal Wheel above Salem, made of shining and beautiful crystals. The light is dazzling and majickal. It draws you right to it, and soon you "land" safely upon the ring. You might see many other people on the ring with you, particularly if visiting on a Thursday night. Some will be priestesses and priests offering help. Others will be there to receive help. You might even recognize specific people.

Many people have filled it with universal light. There is great wisdom and healing in this ring of crystals. Are you here to add to the energy? Or do you have a question or problem? Are you in need of healing? Here you can do the work of the Crystal Wheel. You can request information and answers. The information can come directly in meditation, or the universal mind might guide you in the coming days and weeks to the appropriate resource or person, to give you a detailed answer. But the answer will come.

You can ask for healing for yourself or a loved one. You can feel yourself filling with the light from the circle, or a crystal might direct the majickal light outward to the appropriate recipient. Since it is coming from the ring of crystals, it will not harm you or drain you in any way, and you cannot take on, or leave, any illness at the wheel. The Cabot Tradition always adds this phrase: *"And may it be for the good of all."*

Take as long as you need at the Crystal Wheel. It can be a few minutes or up to an hour. Everyone's needs are unique.

It is now time to return from the Crystal Wheel. Hold the intention of returning to your body. Project your awareness from the wheel, lifting off and traveling with the speed of thought back to your body. Feel yourself become one with your body. When you are ready, give yourself Total Health Clearance and count up from your alpha level.

THE WEAVER OF THE MIDNIGHT SKY

One time when I was teaching in New York City at the shop Enchantments, I was walking through the East Village and came upon an old cast iron fence at a graveyard. The owners of Enchantments sent me a story directly from the crone goddess found in that graveyard, and since then, I have used the story as a meditation on the triple goddess.

Close your eyes and count yourself down into an alpha state. Imagine yourself in a city, walking upon a familiar city street at night. Soak up the sights and sounds, truly feel that you are there. Keep walking in your vision until you enter an area that is unfamiliar to you.

Soon you see a cast iron fence with a gate, blocking off a cemetery or graveyard. The gate is unlocked. You feel drawn to go in. You push it open, and it makes a slow creaking sound as you enter. As you wander among the graves, you hear a noise, a whispering or murmuring.

Soon you come upon an old woman wearing dark blue-black robes. She is sewing. She works at her own pace, and noticing you, looks up. She tells you she is not sewing a cloak, if that is what you are thinking. She continues to stitch, and you notice her needles are like silver crescents.

She looks up again and tells you she is not sewing a death veil or shroud. She keeps sewing, stitch by stitch.

Soon she looks up and says she is sewing the midnight sky. Each needle prick is a star, and the sky is full of stars. She holds up her cloth of the midnight sky, covering herself from your view, and when she lowers it, with her is a young mother and a little girl. She points to the mother and says, "She is the day. She is when work in the world is done."

The mother looks at you. You take a moment and perceive all sorts of thoughts and feelings and images revolving around your work in the world. Are you working in the right way, in harmony with your soul and majick? Do you need to change something in the life that is done during the day? Reflect while she gazes at you, her eyes like reflecting pools.

The old crone then looks to herself and says, "I am the night where all come to rest and make ready for a new day." As she gazes at your, you reflect on your rest and regeneration. Do you care for yourself? Do you rest and rejuvenate, or are you always on the go? Reflect.

Then she looks at the little girl and says, "She is the child of the new day, the morning Sun." You look at the girl, and as she looks back at you, you think about your future hopes, dreams, and plans. Are they right for you? Reflect.

When you are done, the three get up, casting the cloth into the sky. You gaze up and see the stars coming through the needle holes until all you can see is the starry sky of midnight. When you look back again, the three are walking away together, leaving you in the graveyard.

Gaze back upon the midnight sky and reflect upon your life. Go into the stars. Surround yourself with the darkness and the starlight. When done, the images darken, and you can count yourself up from alpha level. Give yourself Total Health Clearance.

Chapter 8: The Elemental Powers

The elements are the fundamental powers of the four directions in the Witch's Circle. We cast circle and call the four quarters and the elemental allies, usually in the form of animals, to anchor these powers in our rituals. Learning to build a relationship with the elements is a powerful way to bring balance and strength to any Witch. The elemental realm also refers beyond the spirits of earth, air, fire, and water and includes faery beings and the spirits of nature. All are powerful allies of the Witch, and worthy of the time and energy necessary to building a relationship with them. Such beings are our friends and companions on the path of majick.

PENNY'S GREEN BALANCE MEDITATION

This is a simple but powerful method to align yourself with the spirit of the five elements through a nature meditation. You can expand upon this work by adding the sound of nature if you cannot go outside. You can incorporate smell by using an oil diffuser with oils of pine or frankincense. You can also use stones, sand, and water to enhance the experience on a tactile level.

Find a comfortable spot where you can do this meditation. You can lie in the grass, or you may also do this indoors lying on the couch or bed. Place a quartz crystal in your left hand and a stone of agate in your right hand. You may also add the elements around the area in which you plan to do this meditation. Place a bowl of water, a piece of tree bark or wood, a feather, a piece of lava rock, and a quartz crystal for water, earth, air, fire, and spirit respectively.

Lie down and place your arms by your sides. Close your eyes and picture yourself lying in a shallow brook in the forest, the water not only covering half of your body, but also flowing from your head down past your feet. Feel the cool water flowing by your sides. Feel the Sun's rays shining on the half of your body above the waterline. Visualize the water below you, the Sun above you, and the forest lining both sides of the brook. Once you have started to smell the green scent of the trees, feel the cool flow of the water under you and the warm sunshine on your face, stomach, and legs. You are ready to count into alpha.

Count down into alpha level. Soon you feel the smooth stones under your body and hear the sounds of this babbling brook as the water passes below you. Smell grass and dirt and the faint scent of pine on the wind. Feel the heat of the Sun mix with a nice cool breeze as it touches your face, chest, stomach, and the top of your legs. You now have all the elements moving with you and around you.

Allow the elements of nature to re-align your body's energies, balancing yin and yang, your negative and positive energies, so that they function as one in perfect harmony, empowering your entire body, strengthening and healing it in perfect balance.

You may remain here as long as you wish, enjoying the environment and continuing to balance your body. Give yourself Total Health Clearance. When you are ready, clear your mind and count up from your alpha state. You should feel refreshed and reenergized.

If you feel you need more grounding, you may place your feet in the dirt. If doing this indoors, you may place your feet on some smooth rocks. You may also put your feet in a warm saltwater bath. Do this meditation as often as you feel you need it. You can never over-meditate with nature.

THE ELEMENT OF EARTH

The element of earth is the power of stability, of solidness and sovereignty. It is the element that contains all the others, for even though all the elements are needed for manifestation, the earth element is the one that brings forth those manifestations in the material world. That is why the pentacle is a symbol for all five elements as well as the element of earth. Working with the element of earth is our quest for security in the physical world, one that ultimately leads to our sense of sovereignty, our true purpose in the world.

Take a favorite stone and place it before you. Light a green candle. Light an earth-scented incense, such as myrrh, patchouli, or vetiver. Relax your body and feel the world beneath your feet. Ask to connect to the element of earth.

Feel the planet Earth beneath your feet. Envision yourself in nature, upon a hill or small mountain on a clear and sunny day. You are standing in the north. Sense the wind and gently passing clouds. Feel the Sun. Feel the living, shifting land beneath you. As you do, in the distance, you hear a rumbling sound. With each moment, it grows stronger, and eventually it sounds like a train or subway coming closer to you. The rumbling earth moves the land beneath you, and while you feel perfectly safe, you can feel the gateway of the earth element opening to you.

A fissure opens up in the land as the earth shakes. The crack opens and allows you to see into the realm of elemental earth.

With the opening of the fissure, the shaking and sound stops. Everything becomes eerily peaceful and serene. Look into the land. See the layers of stone and soil. See the veins of minerals, crystals, and metals running through the land.

Coming up from the fissure are the elemental earth spirits, those beings known as gnomes, for they have the knowledge of the deep earth. These little elemental beings come up and visit with you. They can be playful, but they can also be serious. Sometimes they carry gems, sometimes digging equipment to obtain the gems. They might even give you a gem as a sign of your connection to the element of earth. They may ask for something in return, like asking you to bury something of value as a gift to them.

Ask for the teachings and blessings of elemental earth, and commune with the spirit of the gnomes.

When you are done, thank your elemental allies. They will slowly descend back into the fissure. Remember any promises you have made to them. The fissure begins to rumble once again, but instead of breaking further apart, the crack seals up, as if it were never broken, and the serenity of the mountain hillside is restored.

Take this time to return your awareness to your body, to breathe deep and feel yourself sitting in your meditation chair with the candle burning before you, the stone beside it. Open your eyes. Gaze once more at the candle. When you are ready, rise and take the stone, holding the stone and attuning it with the power of the gnomes who have visited with you.

THE ELEMENT OF AIR

The element of air is the power of communication, creativity, and truth. It is the breath of life, allowing us to connect and communicate with each other. Air brings us knowledge. It helps us learn by clearing away the old and bringing in fresh, new ideas.

Have a feather on a table before you. Light a yellow candle. Burn some aromatic incense, such as lavender, sandalwood, or benzoin, or diffuse an essential oil of lavender or peppermint. Breathe deep, taking in the scent. Close your eyes and relax. Ask to connect to the element of air.

In your mind's eye, gaze up into the sky. See the formation of clouds above you. At first the breeze starts out cool and gentle. You realize you are upon a large hill or mountaintop. You are facing the south, and the big sky is before you as you gaze up. With each moment, the wind grows fiercer, the clouds billowing as they grow bigger and bigger in the sky above.

Listen to the whispers upon the winds. You can hear voices. Secrets are kept in the wind, and you can hear lost wisdom from ages past. Listen deeply and remember.

Upon the wind comes the breath of life. With that life is the presence of the air elementals, known as sylphs. With wings like butterflies or other insects, these small faery-like beings travel with the winds, bringing good news and new ideas.

The wind seems to grow fiercer around you, and soon you feel it lift you up from the ground. The air spirits hold you aloft, and you begin flowing with the wind, looking down upon the earth. As you rise, everything gets smaller and smaller. You start to see the big picture, as if you were a great bird, yet like a hawk or eagle, you can zoom in on anything you want to see closer. What do you see?

The air spirits take you traveling around the world. As you look down, you see scenes of events happening here and now, but the air spirits can also bring you back into the past to see what was, or into the future to think about what might be. As you fly, look around and you'll see exactly what you need to see to find your own deep truth. Sometimes we are shown things we don't want to see, but that we need to see. This is the wisdom of the air elementals.

When your time with the sylphs is done, thank them. They will gently return you back to where you began.

Feel your feet on the ground once more. The winds die down as they say farewell to you. You are back upon the hill, facing the southern sky.

Bring your focus back to your body and where you are sitting. Breathe deep again and find yourself in your chair. The candle and the feather are still before you as you open your eyes. When you are ready, stand up and come to the altar. Hold the feather and fill it with the blessings and energy of the sylphs so that you can use it as a talisman to connect with them whenever you wish.

THE ELEMENT OF FIRE

The element of fire is the power of transformation, passion, and illumination. Fire is the hardest of the elements to understand, as its very nature is change. Fire helps guide us to find our will and inner spark. Fire can warm and cook, but also burn. We must be careful with fire, yet the nature of fire is the nature of majick.

Place a wand before you, for wands hold the light of your majickal will. Place a red candle before you. Burn an incense of dragon's blood or red sandalwood. Some traditions will use a little pure tobacco or spices like coriander and black pepper, but the smoke can be caustic. Light the candle and incense, and then ask to connect to the element of fire. Close your eyes. Breathe deep and attune to the fire burning before you.

With your inner Witch sight, conjure the image of the candle flame in your mind's eye. With each breath, you are feeding the flame, and it grows bigger and brighter, as if there is a burning star before you. The star is not unlike our own Sun, coming up every day over the eastern horizon as it begins its journey. As you look around you, you find yourself on the same familiar hill, facing the east. The light has become the Sun, and the Sun is the fire of your life. It becomes larger and brighter than you have ever seen.

You focus only on the Sun, and its rays reach out to you. Each ray is a fire elemental, a little dragon-like red lizard known as a salamander. While the elementals themselves burn, you are perfectly safe and simply feel their heat upon your skin like a bright sunny day.

Salamanders are the teachers of passion and creativity. They help us attune with our will and purpose in this life. They illuminate our life's path and guide the way in times of darkness. Each of their tiny scales appears to be a flame.

The fire elementals gather before you on the hill, between you and the now-rising Sun in the east. They come together and form a small bonfire. They instruct you to reach within your own heart, head, and belly, and pull out the things that no longer serve your highest good. It might seem strange, but without any harm to you, you can reach inside yourself with this clear intention and find all sorts of things—images, symbols, pictures, words, or feelings—that need to come out.

What do you pull from your heart that no longer serves your highest good? Throw them all into the fire before you.

What do you pull from your head that no longer serves your highest good? Throw all of these things into the fire of the salamanders before you. The fire grows larger before you with all this fuel.

What do you pull from your belly that no longer serves your highest good? Again, throw that which is unnecessary into the fire. The fire blazes brighter than it's ever been.

The light of the fire radiates into you, filling you with energy. You feel a level of life force, of vitality, that you didn't know you had. You feel your passion and your power as you watch the fire.

The fire burns out and reveals the salamanders playfully frolicking around in the ashes. Look into the ashes. What do you see?

With that last message, say farewell to your fire elemental friends. They seem to simply return once again into the light of the Sun, as you notice it's gone quite far on its journey towards the west during the course of this "day." While you stand on the hillside facing the east, you realize it's time to return.

Feel the chair where you are sitting and your body resting comfortably in the chair. Feel your fingers and toes, and bring your awareness back. As you open your eyes, you see your candle and your wand. Come back fully and rise. Hold the wand and charge it with the fire blessings of vitality. It will help you return to your elemental fire connection whenever you need it.

THE ELEMENT OF WATER

The element of water is the power of love, compassion, and healing. Water flows just as our emotions flow. Water helps us get in touch with our feelings and dissolve away emotional blocks where our feelings have stagnated, bringing us healing and renewal.

Place a majick chalice or other special cup full of water before you. If you don't have one, use a seashell. Burn a blue or sea-green candle. Burn some jasmine or mugwort incense or diffuse some Ylang Ylang essential oil. Breathe deep, into your belly. Feel the flow of air in and out of your body. Start at the bottom of your lungs, then fill your middle lungs, and then the top of your lungs. As you exhale, exhale out from the top, middle, and bottom of the lungs, creating a rolling wave of breath within your body. This will help relax your body and get you into a deeper meditative state. When you are ready, mentally ask to connect to the element of water.

Feel the water within your body, the flow of blood pumping with your heart. Feel the gurgling of the stomach. Remember that your body is made from water. Close your eyes. Listen for the sound of ocean waves. You can hear them. In your mind's eye, see the shore in the distance. Hear the rolling waves come crashing in and the sound of sea birds upon the shore. You find yourself on the familiar hillside, facing the west where the shore is. You walk down the hilltop towards the sea line. The waves lap against your bare feet, cool to the touch.

As you gaze out into the blue, open seas, you see them. Playing in the water just beyond the ninth wave are the mermaids. Known as undines by magicians and alchemists, they are the spirits of water, the teachers and healers of the realm of elemental water. They are the elemental faeries of the deep seas.

You move a little deeper into the water to see them better, but they are elusive. They dive deep. One motions to the right of your position, to a rocky outcropping where the sea and the stones meet. Intuitively, you know you must go there.

You make your way out to the rocks and walk carefully to their edge, balancing upon the rocks to get to the westernmost point. There is a little grotto of rocks where the waters pool, sheltered a bit from the open sea. There you sit and wait, dangling your legs into the water, watching the light reflect off the surface of the blue seas before you.

Soon the surface is disturbed by movement from beneath. Bursting through the surface of the water come several mermaids. These water elementals greet you and welcome you to their shore.

The water elementals teach how the source of all life upon the world is water. They speak of the healing and blessing properties of water—seas, rivers, ponds, lakes, and even swamps. There are mysteries in the water.

The elementals begin to pour water from the sea over your head. They ask you to think about your greatest sorrow. As you reflect upon that sorrow, the water flows over you, over your heart, and back into the endless sea, taking with it the pain, but leaving the lesson with you.

The mermaids ask you to reflect upon your greatest joy, and likewise the water flows over your heart. But this time, your joy empowers the water and blesses the water for everyone. Sorrows are shared to be dissipated. Joys are multiplied to bless.

Lastly, they ask you to think of your deepest love. And as they pour the water over you, the love becomes the more divine compassion, and compassion flows into the world.

Commune about your sorrows, joys, and loves with the mermaids.

When you feel your time is complete, thank the undine water spirits. They thank and bless you, and then return to the seas.

You get up from the rocks and make your way back to the main shore, and from there, up to the hilltop where you began. You look at the Sun setting upon the western sea, feeling its warmth upon you and the warmth that is in your heart, and you are blessed.

Feel your skin dry in the sunlight. When you are ready, begin your return by bringing your full awareness back to your body. Continue to breathe deep, but open your eyes. With eyes open, you gaze at the candle and the cup or shell. You rise and hold the tool, infusing it with the blessings of the water elementals, and it will become a tool for you to work more deeply with the water elements in the future.

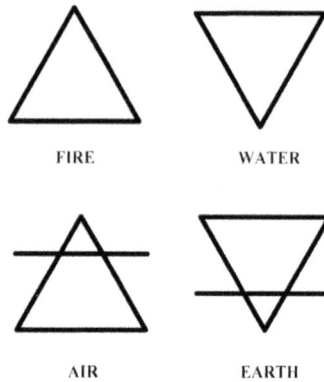

Fig. 3: Elemental Triangles

THE FAERY REALM

The faery realm is the realm of enchantment. It is another dimension where our elder cousins live. Faeries are creatures of fate and creatures of nature, born in a time when the world was much younger, before humanity as we know it today.

Faeries can be guides and allies to those who keep the old ways. Many Witches have a kinship to faeries, and in some way, we carry the faery blood. You can seek out the faeries and try to build a relationship with them.

Light a green or blue candle. If elecampane, a faery herb also known as elfwort or elfdock, is available to you, scatter some around the candle. Gaze into the candle and hold the intention of finding the faeries in a manner that is safe and good for you. Sometimes faeries are known as tricksters, and often have a very different moral code than humans, doing harm because they don't operate under the same conditions as humanity. But when we approach them with respect, they can be great allies.

Find yourself on the edge of a faery forest. You make your way from a meadow of wildflowers, rich in their scent and vibrant in their colors, to the tree line at the edge of the woods. To find the faery folk, you know you'll have to go into the deep forest.

You take notice of the bark of the trees, the color and shape of it. Reach out and touch the first few trees, asking permission of the tree guardians to enter the space. As you do, you can smell the forest, the pine and the musty decay on the forest floor. You feel the trees give you permission to enter, and as you walk the dense path into the forest, you can hear the scurrying of little animals. They become aware of your presence.

As you walk, take particular notice of the ferns on the forest floor as they brush up against you. The roots of the largest trees are gnarled and tangled, digging deep into the Earth.

With each step, less and less light filters into the forest, and the realm becomes darker. With each step into the deep woods, the light moves from twilight to nighttime. You can barely see your feet in front of you as you walk, so you move much more slowly, sensing and feeling your way more than seeing. Be sure not to trip over any roots or rocks.

Soon you feel a tree, and you know this tree is special. You place your hands on it and make your way to sit down at the base of the tree with your back to the trunk. You take a moment to rest, to feel, and to breathe with the tree. With each moment, you become more like the tree. What little of the night sky you can see through the canopy of trees is filled with stars. They shine down upon you from the midnight blue sky.

With the stars above, you sense a sparkle of light among the trees, as if little stars are dancing in the forest. The sparkle of light seems to hide from you when you focus on it, ducking around the silhouetted trees, yet it still moves towards you. Soon it moves behind a tree next to you.

A face peeks out around the tree and looks at you with a grin. You discover the light is a wood faery. She has come to greet you. As soon as she does, she again transforms into a will o' the wisp light and moves deeper into the forest, beckoning you.

Will you go deeper?

If you follow the faery light, you find yourself guided safely through the dark woods. Soon in the distance, you see a brighter blue-white light, and you know that is where you are headed. The wisp guides you to a clearing. A fire burns there, like a campfire but with a fountain of blue faery light, and a group of larger faerie beings have gathered around it. They invite you to their light. Remember the old prohibition to never drink or eat anything from the faery realm, but take this time to commune with the faeries around the fire. They are dancing and singing. They may share faery secrets with you. Be respectful as you would with beloved elders. Keep on your best behavior, even when declining any refreshments.

The dawn is coming, and your faery friends must retreat back beneath the hills and mounds. The wood faery who guided you in will gently guide you back to the path, taking the form of the will o' the wisp again. Say your farewells and return. The light is dappling through the canopy of leaves, guiding you. Shafts of light come in as the Sun rises, and your faery guide withdraws as the beams of light illuminate the forest floor. You recognize where you are and walk the path back to the edge of the forest, remembering your time with the faery folk. Walk out of the forest and back into the meadow. Return. Become aware of your body and your heartbeat. Return your awareness to here and now and open your eyes. Snuff the candle and scatter the herbs.

ROWAN TREE MEDITATION

In Irish folklore and history, the rowan tree is sacred to the faery realm and guarded by yellow cats. Its berries, if bestowed as a gift from the fae, bring youth and rejuvenation. Penny created the Rowan Tree Meditation for such revitalization, and due to the faery associations with rowan trees, you can also use it to find your own faery guide.

Sit in a comfortable place and count down into alpha level. As you feel the stress of the day leave your body, you begin to relax all your muscles and exhale as you go deeper into alpha level. It is a clear day. Feel the warm summer breeze and the Sun on your face. Hear the rustling of the leaves. Look around you and envision rolling hills, plush and green, and a blue sky above. Thirty feet in front of you is a tree, its branches thick with clusters of red berries, some dropping to the ground as the branches sway in the wind. At the base of the tree, you see a yellow-orange tabby cat. This is one of three guardians of the rowan tree. Now look up. In the top branches, you see two more cats, each identical to the first, one to the left and one to the right.

Visualize in your hand three mojo bags. Using your hands, raise them to the Sun, allowing the Sun's rays once again to warm your face as its rays also bless the three bags. Visualize yourself bending forward and giving the first gift to the cat at the bottom of the tree. He rubs happily against your leg and purrs. Visualize yourself rising up to the top of the tree. Hand your gift to the cat on the left. He purrs happily at your offering. Turn to the cat on the right and make your third offering.

Now that you have pleased the guardians, ask their permission to have one berry. See the three cats nodding in approval. Take the berry from the top of the tree and feel yourself floating slowly back down to the ground. Visualize yourself eating this berry and feel the blessing of the faery spread all throughout your body. Rejuvenate! As the energy of the berry passes through your body, you feel revitalized and youthful.

Stay in this moment and enjoy the splendor as this energy moves through your body and mind, giving you mental clarity and bodily vigor. See the energy emanate from the berry in the center of your stomach, the solar plexus chakra point. Envision the energy spreading outward throughout the body, correcting and healing as it goes, passing through your elbows and knees, working its way to your fingertips, toes, and the top of your head. Hold this berry at your solar plexus chakra point in your mind. You may now place your right hand over your solar plexus, covering the berry within. You may use this to call upon the fae to guide you in your majickal workings. You may also do this to revitalize yourself with clarity of mind and body, or use the energy of youth to repair joints and muscle. Keep this berry in your belly. You may revisit this space anytime; simply place your hand over the berry to activate its majick. When you are ready to finish, place your hand down next to your side and clear your mind of all images and thoughts. Relax. Give yourself Total Health Clearance and count up from alpha level.

LORD OF THE FOREST

The Lord of the Forest is the god who rules over the life of the forest. He is often depicted in old carvings as a Green Man with a leaf face. He is a god of life and light, just as the trees reach up to the light of the sky. He is balanced, for the roots of the forest also grow deep and into the dark. He teaches us the ways of life and balance.

Fig. 4: The Green Man

To prepare for this vision, light a green candle. You can anoint the candle or your own wrists with a drop of oakmoss, patchouli, or pine essential oil. If you have an oak leaf, hold it before the flame and gaze at the shadow it casts. Recite this spell, place the leaf before the candle, close your eyes, and prepare to visit the Lord of the Forest.

Let me grow like your trees
My feet grounded and balanced on earth.
May my arms reach to the sky
And draw down creative thought.
May my growth bring abundance,
Joy, and peace to Earth
And peace in my home.
So mote it be.

Imagine the blue sky above you. Smell the clean, crisp air. White wispy clouds pass through the sky, and as you bring your gaze down, you see the tree line of an ancient forest. The dark green hues of the forest filled with oak, ash, pine, and hawthorn seem to glow from within. You feel the presence of something powerful and ancient within the forest and walk towards the path visible in the tree line, entering the forest realm.

As you walk upon the path, the dry leaves crunch beneath your feet, and you smell the fertile earth of life and decay. The Sun is dappled through the branches, illuminating the path with spots of sunlight amid the cool darkness.

You enter deeper into the forest and feel drawn to a presence. And there, you see him. There is the Green Man, the Lord of the forest. He invites you over to him. His presence is immense. You can feel the life force rippling off his leafy face.

He has you stand tall, strong, like a tree. You reach up with your arms towards the sky, like branches. Soon you feel as if you are becoming the tree. Your feet grow like roots and become grounded upon the Earth. The energy of the Earth flows into your roots, into the trunk of your body, and balances you. Your arms reach up to the sky, and as you reach into the sky, you draw down this creative energy, inspiring you. Like a tree, you embody abundance, joy, and peace on the Earth. You are a part of Mother Earth as you are guided by the Lord of the Forest. Breathe here with the forest.

The Green Man touches you, and you shapeshift from a tree to your human self once again. Give thanks to the Lord of the Forest and follow the path back through the woods, bringing the peace of the forest back to your home.

Return your awareness to the room and gaze at the green candle. Ground yourself back in this world. Let the candle burn if you can, to continue the Lord of the Forest's blessing, or snuff it out to relight again when you want to commune with him.

While we traditionally see this figure as a Green Man, during the second year I was living in Salem, Massachusetts, I experienced this meditation as becoming the Green Woman. The spontaneous journey was a bit spooky, but also exciting to be at one with the forest. The vines went up my legs and into my body. I was covered in leaves and blossoming with flowers. At first I felt tangled up in it, but once I relaxed into the vision, I got to see what it was like to be the Green Woman myself.

EARTH HEALING MEDITATION

This meditative and immersive ritual, created by Penny, requires one cup of sea water, one bowl of natural soil from outdoors (not bagged potting soil), one feather foraged from the ground, and one found penny.

Place the copper coin and the feather to the left of your body, the ocean water and earth soil on the right. Lie down in a comfortable spot, indoors or outdoors, and count down into your alpha state. Envision the feather on the screen of your mind. Turn it around and look at it, examining all sides. Envision behind it the beautiful blue sky dotted with small white clouds drifting across the sky. Raise your left hand and make an erasing motion as you speak:

I wipe away impurities. My atmosphere is healed.
I wipe away impurities. My stratosphere is healed.

Envision the feather again, seeing it glow with white light energy, and speak:

The sky is healed as it was, as it shall be! It is fixed!

Next envision the copper penny on the screen of your mind. Turn it around, looking at both sides, and know this coin represents the element of fire. Now we envision ourselves leaving the sky and descending lower and lower, down to the grass line. Then we descend lower into the Earth itself, descending through its layers, through its bedrock. You start to feel warm as you descend closer to the heart of Mother Earth. You begin to see the orange hue of the magma and feel its warmth. Raise your hand again, and with an erasing motion, speak:

Great Mother Earth, your blood is healed. I remove all impurities. May your blood flow as it was, as it should be! It is fixed!

Next we move to the Earth's surface symbolized by the soil. Envision the bowl of soil on your screen, turning it and looking at the soil from all angles. Now see the earth above the bedrock, brown and rich. Travel up through the layers, looking at the different colors of soil as you pass through geological timelines. The soil gets darker, and you start to see tree roots framed by a small layer of grass roots traveling horizontally across your screen. Raise both hands, and in a crumbling motion, run both hands through the soil, feeling its texture. Some is sand-like, and some is rich with moisture. Now move your hand in an erasing motion and speak:

I purify this soil. This soil is balanced and healed.
This soil is as it should be and always will be! It is fixed!

Next we envision our bowl of ocean water. See the minerals and ocean particles floating within it. Visualize its motion in the sea. Now see yourself rising up and out of the soil. Rise up to the blue sky high above the trees. Look down to one side and see a shoreline and the wide-open ocean. Travel over to it. Pass the shore and continue out until you are over the ocean. Look around until you cannot see land. Now turn three hundred and sixty degrees, seeing nothing but ocean. See yourself traveling down into the water. Continue down until you start to see ocean plants. Look up to see the sunlight sending beams of light down into the water. Under your feet you see sand, and off to the right, rocks covered with waving seaweed and barnacles. You see communities of periwinkles clustered on the rock. Listen to the movement of the water and watch as the fish slowly swim by with no fear. Raise your hand, and with an erasing motion, speak the words:

The ocean is healed. Its pH is balanced, and all that live within are healthy. I remove all impurities.
This water is as it should be and always will be! It is fixed!

Next we rise out of the ocean up into the blue sky. Feel the Sun's rays on your face as its warmth dries your body. Travel back to the spot where you started, hovering over the land, looking at the blue sky. As you feel joy and contentment fill your body, bring all four items you have collected onto the screen of your mind: feather, coin, bowl of water, and the bowl of soil. Envision them spinning in a circle faster and faster until they all become one. As they do so, the items turn into a ball of brilliant white light. Visualize this light getting brighter and brighter until it explodes in a burst of sparkles, millions of sparkling bits. See the sparkles coming down and settling on the trees, the grass, and the ocean. Envision every leaf sparkling with white light, like glitter in the Sun. As you speak the words, see this white light absorbed into everything. As it is absorbed and disappears, speak:

The Earth is healed. She is as she was, as she should be! It is fixed!

You may stay here as long as you wish. When you are ready, give yourself Total Health Clearance and count yourself up from alpha level. Take your items and return them all to the ocean to carry the healing outward across the world.

HEALING WATER

Witches have always known what researcher and author Masaru Emoto has explored in *Messages from Water* and his other books: water is influenced by the thoughts and emotions projected into it. This concept is one of the key ideas of our potions, where majickal intention is placed into water, along with corresponding herbs and oils, to hold that intention. Emoto's work focuses on pure water, and how intentions, conscious or unconscious, can influence the shape, vitality, and health of the water. Since reading his work, I have focused even more on working with bottles of clear water for my own health and the health of others.

Emoto's work shows that words spoken and sung, prayed silently, or even written and placed upon a bottle or bowl, will change the energy and patterns of the water. To meditate and program the water in your own bottle, try the following:

Take the label off the bottle. If you can take the water out of a plastic bottle and use clean glass, all the better, but this also works within plastic bottles. Just use a clear bottle and make sure all writing is taken off it.

Write your intention on the bottle, such as the word "Heal" if you are ill or "Healthy" if you want to maintain health.

Shut everything down around you that would distract you. Shut off computers and phones. Turn off lights. Make everything as quiet as possible.

Go into your meditative alpha state while holding the bottle.

Start by connecting to the water, feeling the water in the bottle in your hands. Then focus on the love and thankfulness for water. Without water, there would be no life or health.

Project into the water the intention of healing the human body, restoring one hundred percent health and vitality.

Return from alpha and let the water settle somewhere peaceful for at least twelve hours. Drink the water to continue to heal. Repeat with all your water throughout the day.

According to these teachings, it takes a full twelve hours, and possibly up to twenty-four, for the water to accept the program. So once you have done this work, wait at least twelve hours before drinking it to experience the full effect. Some keep the water in the refrigerator with the intention word still on the bottle. Others will include things like sacred geometry designs or place stones into the water, but to start, I recommend just using water and a simple intentional word. I try to always keep a bottle ready to drink.

You can also expand upon this idea and program the water in your body regularly to increase health. Follow the same procedure above, but when you are focused on your love and thankfulness for water, continue outward into the world and your own body. Think about how the world is roughly three-fourths water, as are our bodies, for all our cells contain water. Then follow these instructions:

Envision the water in your body, in every cell of your body. Just like programming the water in the bottle, program the water in every cell to heal your body on all levels. Affirm you will be healed of any and all illness, restoring one hundred percent health and vitality.

Focus on anywhere there is pain or illness. Focus on the water there. Program the water to heal you completely. Move through your body, starting with the bones and connective tissue. Then move into the soft tissue. Explore the organs. Envision the water in your entire body healing you and restoring health on all levels. Move through the kidneys, pancreas, liver, heart, and lungs. Envision the blood and the blood vessels, the nerves and spine, all healed. Feel the water traveling into your face, your eyes, and your brain. As the water travels through your body, everything it touches is healed.

Return from alpha and let the healing settle within your body. Remember it can take up to twelve hours, or even more, before you truly get the full benefit from this work.

When I started this practice, I was having a lot of health difficulties, and I couldn't stand well. Soon after programming my water, I could stand by leaning on something, and then without leaning. Soon I was walking the halls. I still have some pain at times, but I am much better than I was before I began this practice of programming my water for healing.

In the Green Ministry of the Cabot Kent Hermetic Temple, we experimented with this technique for the gardens, focusing on both sunflowers and pumpkins. One gallon had the word "Grow" on the bottle, while the other had "Complete Growth" on it. We kept the bottles in a quiet, peaceful place for over twelve hours with the words on them. We then used them to water the plants. Both were exceptionally larger than the ones that used regular water, but they didn't stay that way for long, showing that the process would need to be repeated to continue to have results.

OCEAN MEDITATION

This meditation was created by Penny for the Green Ministry of the Cabot Tradition and is for those who live by the ocean or who can get to the ocean. To perform it, you will require a small one-to-two-dram bottle that can be sealed.

> Simply go to the ocean with the small bottle to meditate on healing and cleaning the ocean. Take a dram (twenty drops) or two of ocean water. Hold the bottle and conjure the feeling of deep gratitude, love, and care for the ocean. With this feeling in your heart, program the water in your bottle for purification of all pollutants in the ocean.

> Count down into alpha while holding the bottle and feeling the love in your heart. Charge the water for purification of the waters all around the world. Use the word "purification" as a mantra. Charge the water to be pure and healthy. Charge the water to transform the consciousness of humanity, of the world, to stop

the pollution of the waterways and seas. Charge this water to act upon all the waters of the world.

As you do, envision the whole ocean where you are, the entire seacoast. Then cast your mind out to all of the seas and oceans, to all of the waterways that feed them. Envision all of the waters of the world. Charge them to be pure.

When you are done, count up from alpha. You can either pour the water back into the sea or take it home with you and repeat this process with the small bottle for a few days, a week, or even a month, strengthening the intention. Then return it to the sea to do its majick.

If you are moved to do so, gather a group together and go down to the edge of the ocean and sit and meditate, doing this work to cleanse it. As a group, ask the water to be pure and healthy. To help your visualization, you can get a map of the world so that you can look at all the different oceans and seas across the globe. This meditation can also be done with a pond, a stream, a lake, or a river. Eventually the waters will make their way to the ocean through flow, evaporation, and precipitation.

Chapter 9: Egyptian Visions

While the Cabot Tradition is rooted in the myths and gods of my Celtic ancestors, I have a deep and personal relationship with the land of Egypt. Strong past life memories combined with Celtic links (through the story of Queen Scota of Scotland, who claimed Egyptian descent) bring the Egyptian gods close to my heart. The goddess Isis in particular has been a strong ally and guide in my life, and the Hermetic Principles of *The Kyballion*, a modern distillation of Hermetic philosophy and Egyptian wisdom by three anonymous initiates, has been a guiding force in my own life and teachings. No matter your own path, the gods of Egypt embody a wisdom and love that can help anyone find the majick in their own life.

One boon in working with the Egyptian deities is that many of their icons and statues have survived, and reproductions of these relics can easily be found. The traditional images resonate with the old gods very well, much more so than the new images and statues. If you obtain a statue, you bring the energy of that god into your space, and you can work with it through the statues. Painting the statues gold—or even better, with gold leaf paint—helps align them with the Egyptian Sun majick. You can also anoint them with oils, or leave out offerings of candles, incense, and for very traditional practitioners, food. I speak to each statue individually, every morning. I address them and honor them in some way, even if it is quick. I tell them I love them and thank them for all of their help over the years. They have given me the love of the otherworld. Isis taught me the reality of the otherworld, and far before I ever spoke to the dead, she was the first goddess to speak to me.

THOTH-HERMES AND THE EMERALD TABLET

The philosopher god Hermes Trismegistus is typically equated with the messenger god of the Greeks, Hermes, and his Roman counterpart, Mercury, but in many ways, he is more closely associated with the Egyptian god we know as Thoth, who was known to the Egyptians as Tehuti. He may be a universal Indo-European god who taught the basic tenets of civilization and science, and he established the mystery schools that informed the Druids and the teachings of Pythagoras. Caesar said the Celts of Gaul worshipped their own form of Mercury (who might have been the Gaulish Lug) as a god of many skills and talents. In alchemy and Hermetic teachings, the giver of civilization and majick is known as Hermes Trismegistus, or Hermes thrice greatest or thrice wise.

Hermes is associated with the Emerald Tablet, an ancient artifact with the mysteries of alchemy carved upon it, surviving from a time before the Great Flood. Today we meditate upon the image of our own personal Emerald Tablet to gain access to ancient wisdom and solve problems in our own lives by applying such wisdom.

To connect with Thoth-Hermes, light a green candle, and if you have a green stone, ideally an emerald, place it before the candle. Gaze upon the green color, and when ready, close your eyes to seek the mystery of the Emerald Tablet.

Feel the cool breeze upon your cheeks and the motion of moving forward with a gentle sway. Picture yourself in an ancient boat, floating down a river. The Sun shines down upon you, and while hot, it is not uncomfortable. It feels good. The flowing water lulls you into a gentle state of relaxation, and you sail mysteriously down the river.

As you look all around you, there are fertile shores of greenery, and in the distance, the yellow-brown sand of the desert. In the distance, down the river, is the outline of a magnificent building, a temple. Though there is no one piloting your boat, it is majickally led to the shore.

Instinctively you step out and follow the well-groomed path from the shoreline to the temple gate. The temple naturally leads you into a central chamber, but as you gaze at each side, you realize this temple is like a library, with many scrolls and ancient writings carved into its walls. This is a place of learning.

You enter the main chamber and see a figure. It's a man dressed in white. This is the thrice-great Hermes himself, here to greet you. From the shadows come other figures, teachers, and wise ones from across the world, women and men. You think you see Pythagoras as well as some Druids. The figures welcome you to this temple of learning. Tell them your name and explain to them you seek knowledge for the good of all.

They take you to the far end of the temple. You pass through a gate with two pillars, black on the left and white on the right. The pillars are covered with mysterious symbols and inscriptions that seem somehow familiar, but you can't read them. Once you are through, you see a structure the size of a large bookcase, covered in a white cloth. Thoth-Hermes pulls off the cloth and reveals the giant Emerald Tablet. It is etched with scripts of symbols, like the pillars, but they move, dance, and disappear. One moment it is smooth and clearly faceted. Other times it appears to have writing upon it. It radiates a powerful green energy into the temple. You can see why they cover it when it's not in use. It feels almost overwhelming.

One of the wise teachers majickally reaches into the Emerald Tablet and pulls out a small duplicate the size of your hand. It is a rectangular piece of mineral, bright green, also carved with symbols. The back has a point to it. It contains all the information you need. The guide places it in the palm of your left hand, point down. The emerald embeds itself in your palm, but causes no pain. It feels quite natural to be there. It feels good. The point comes out of the back of your hand and warms to your touch. You can gaze into the surface. The carved symbols dance upon it as if they were alive, forming a smooth surface for you to gaze into, like gazing into a mirror.

The guide explains you have all the knowledge you need in the palm of your hand. Ask a question, and the emerald will reveal the answer. It can also heal you with its emerald-green energy. Gaze into the emerald in your palm and ask it a question. It will answer you truly.

Sometimes the information will not come immediately, but the emerald will guide you to the necessary resources—including people, books, and other media—to answer your questions and present you with the solution. The emerald tries to find ways you can hear and understand it.

The guides let you ask any final questions you have on the use of the emerald. Be sure to thank them all and also Thoth-Hermes. When you are done, one guides you back out of the temple, telling you that you can return when you need help, but reminding you that the emerald is a touchstone for all their wisdom. You say good-bye and enter the boat again. As if piloted by an invisible driver, the boat then launches into the waters of the river, and you flow gently under the Sun. You enter a cool mist and find your awareness returning back to your body, here and now. Gently open your eyes and extinguish the green candle. Ground and balance yourself as necessary. While you can use the stone upon the altar, the true emerald tablet is still psychically embedded in your hand and is available anytime you need it.

The Temple of Isis

Isis is the Egyptian form of the Great Mother, though her worship spread far beyond Egypt. She is the sister-wife to Osiris, now the Lord of the Underworld, and mother to the avenging hawk-headed god Horus. Together they made the primary family of Egyptian mythology.

One of Isis' myths, along with resurrecting her husband-brother to conceive their son, is tricking Ra into revealing his secret name, the true name of the Sun, allowing her to gain power over all things. Much like in the myth of Rumpelstiltskin, Isis can help you find a name or word of power from the gods to empower your own majick. There are many things Isis the magician can teach a Witch willing to listen.

The Temple of Isis meditation can be done separately or as a part of the Egyptian Sun Meditation as found in **Chapter Four**. Start by lighting a white candle in honor of her. If you have any lapis lazuli or carnelian, place either or both before the candle, as these stones are sacred to this goddess.

Breathe deep. Relax. Close your eyes. Cast your mind back to an ancient time and place, to the land of Khemet, to Egypt. Draw yourself to the flowing Nile and the desert sands. Look up into the sky and see two great white pillars looming above you. From behind you flutter the black doves of Isis, moving past you and upward, toward the gate between the two pillars. As they enter, a deep-blue light emanates from the temple. You rise like a black dove, flying up and entering the light.

You find yourself in the Temple of Isis. The great goddess is there before you, upon her golden throne. Isis wears the crown of the golden disc. Light pours down through an opening in the temple, and the light strikes the disk upon her head and illuminates you and the entire temple.

Isis rises and spreads her golden wings outward. She steps forward, towards you. She wraps her wings around you and whispers, *"napu kanapu rah, napu kanapu rah, napu kanapu rah,"* over and over again to you.

She holds you and flies up with you in her arms. You fly up and out of the temple into the clear sky with the goddess. As she flies with you, she may whisper more secrets in your ear. You survey the ancient world, all from above. She points out places of power and deep mysteries.

As you fly, you feel the flow of love, life, and majick between you and the goddess. You feel that energy build within you, creating a blessing from the great lady who holds the secret name of Ra.

Slowly she returns through the roof of the temple and returns to the main chamber. She releases you gently, returning you once more to the floor, and steps back upon her golden throne. She bids you farewell.

Follow the path back from the temple, through the white pillars, and back to where you began.

The Tomb of Osiris

As Isis is seen as the Great Mother of the Egyptian pantheon, Osiris is the great father. He is the brother and husband to Isis, which can seem strange to us, but in the ancient myths, siblings often married. Their special family had five siblings, including Osiris, Isis, Set, Nephthys, and Horus the Elder. The ruling god Ra feared future rivals and was angry to find that the sky goddess Nuit was pregnant with five children. He forbade her from giving birth on any day of the year. The god of wisdom, Thoth, knew the children needed to be born, so he gambled with the Moon god Konshu. Every time Konshu lost, he had to give Thoth some of his moonlight, almost rivaling the light of Ra. With that light, Thoth constructed five new days, one for each of the new gods, and these days fell nowhere on the days of the year. This created five extra days in the Egyptian calendar when these gods were born, and they turned out to be some of the most pivotal and important of the Egyptian pantheon, ushering in a new age. Their birth angered Ra, who forever more separated Nuit from her husband the Earth god Geb. Eventually Osiris became a ruler of the gods as Ra receded from leadership, eventually being succeeded by his son with Isis, Horus the Younger.

In the tale of Isis and Osiris, their brother Set, a god of chaos and destruction, is jealous of their power and status. He traps Osiris in the first coffin, built to his exact specifications. As part of a party game, Set has everyone try it out. The one who fit perfectly in it would "win" it. None fits it quite right until Osiris. Once Osiris is in the coffin, Set and his accomplices seal it and float it down the river, where it eventually becomes part of a tree that grows around it. The tree is later made into a pillar of the palace of the king of Byblos. Isis finds Osiris' body there and resurrects him for the first time. In some versions of the myth, she is then impregnated by him before he expires again. In others, he is murdered for a second time before fathering a child. In all versions, Set then attacks Osiris, cutting his body into fourteen pieces and scattering them all across Egypt. Isis manages to find all but one, the phallus, and in some versions, she fashions a majickal phallus for him that allows her to become pregnant with their son, Horus. Osiris is reborn as the lord of the underworld. Horus goes on to battle his uncle for control over Egypt.

Because of his trials, Osiris is a god of the dead and the underworld. He can help us connect with loved ones who have passed. Personally, I see Osiris as a god of protection who can expect the unexpected dangers, even from loved ones. I call upon him whenever going into large crowds, concerts, or during travel. He can alert you to any problem and help you take action before it becomes a danger to you.

You can use this meditation to connect to Osiris. Like the Temple of Isis, it can be preceded by the Egyptian Sun meditation in **Chapter Four**. Light a white or green candle in honor of Osiris. His symbols are the crook and flail. Some Witches use the wand and athame instead, crossing them before the candle to symbolize the two powers of Osiris.

Unlike other meditations, for this one I suggest you lie down like a mummy, with your feet together and your arms crossed over your chest, in what some call the God Position when performed standing. This emulates the pose of Osiris and can help you connect to him, while simultaneously directing your energy inwards.

Relax your body. Breathe deep in and out and feel the breath rise and fall within your body. Close your eyes. Draw your mind back to the ancient past, to the majickal lands of Egypt, where the mysteries are kept in the sacred temples and tombs. Cast your mind back to a sacred valley where kings and queens are buried. In the hillside many gates are hidden, protecting the tombs of the ancient leaders of this great land.

One gate calls out to you, and you approach it. The wind of the desert blows all around you, and you feel rushed to get inside, to shelter yourself from any coming storm. The gates open for you, and you find yourself entering a long dark tunnel, lit by flickering torches. The flames illuminate walls carved and painted with hieroglyphic drawings, not in dull stone, but vibrant colors. As you walk, you notice the pictures and symbols seem to tell the story of Osiris and Set, the green and red gods, brothers battling for the throne. You see the magnificent image of Isis, painted in blue and white, and the resurrection of Osiris in the blackness of the underworld.

In the distance is a doorway outlined in a green light. The air grows cooler as you approach it. You enter the green light and find yourself in the Tomb of Osiris. There he sits as pharaoh upon a throne, with the pharaonic crown on his head, crook and flail in hand. Within the chamber you see his sarcophagus, opened. Four canopic jars containing the organs of life are also in the chamber; the prototypes of these jars would later be depicted with the heads of the jackal god Anubis or the four sons of Horus.

You kneel before Osiris, and he uncrosses his arms. He places his shepherd's crook, used to guide his flock, upon one shoulder and his flail, used to separate the chaff from the grains, upon the other. You feel the twin blessings pour into you, the active and the passive, the two aspects of polarity. You feel as if you are being taken apart, and all that is not for your highest good falls away.

Osiris rises and leads you to the sarcophagus. He anoints you with myrrh oil and begins to wrap you and bandage you, not unlike a mummy. You lie down in the coffin, and he slowly closes the lid. The soft green light of the temple tomb gives way to darkness, and you dwell in the darkness. Everything becomes silent.

You feel as if you are floating upon the Nile, floating in darkness. Someone repeatedly whispers into your ear, "Osiris is a Black God," and you soon understand. The blackness is the blackness of death, but also blackness of the fertile earth and the depths of the holy waters. You focus upon who you want to be when you are reborn. What have you left behind in your old life? What no longer serves? What seeds now have room to grow within you? When you rise from the waters, what will you be? When you burst forth like a new stalk talking root, who will you be?

As you float and dream, you begin to see points of light above you. Soon you realize you are floating on the Nile, looking up at the stars. One by one, the stars come into focus from the pure blackness. Your eyes focus on the three stars of Orion's belt, and you feel them shining down upon you, filling you with their light. You may see other stars, such as Sirius, the star of Isis, or any other stars that shine their blessing upon you.

As the dawn begins in the east, the sky starts to fill with light. And at the same time, the coffin lid is slowly opened, and you see the shining face of Osiris greet you. He takes you by the right hand and lifts you up out of the coffin, reborn as the new self you have dreamed. Feel the love between you and the good god Osiris. Feel yourself like a newborn, ready to start a new day. Osiris blesses you and sends you forth out of his tomb and through the hall. You return to the valley of the kings where you began. You return and awaken to the world, reborn and arisen.

FLYING WITH HORUS

Horus is the divine child of Isis and Osiris, nephew to Set and Nephthys. When Osiris died and was reborn as the lord of the underworld, Horus assumed the battle with Set, his uncle, in place of his father. Eventually, after much hardship and trials, he was victorious and assumed leadership of Egypt, eventually leading to the pharaonic succession of human rulers of the ancient land.

In history, there have been many forms of Horus documented by Egyptologists, often conflicting. Confusion sometimes arises over the tales of Horus the Elder, often a sibling to Osiris and Isis, and Horus the Younger, their child. Sometimes he is equated with, or another form of, both Osiris and Ra. Usually he is a god of warriors, hunters, pharaohs, and the sky.

In a meditation I share with you, I spontaneously became Horus. I shapeshifted into his hawk form by putting his head upon my head. Horus' divine body became like a vehicle for my remote viewing experiences. With his help, I could get there faster and have the protection, vision, and insight of a god, which is immensely helpful when traveling to difficult or distant places. Sometimes our human consciousness needs help and protection in unusual environments, particularly those far from Earth. Try asking Horus for help when doing remote viewing and psychic travel journeys.

Fig. 5: Horus as the Hawk

First focus upon a location, physical or spiritual, that could be difficult for you to visit psychically on your own. What location could Horus help you reach safely? It can be a place in history, in the past or future. It could be a location here upon Earth now, or a spiritual realm or temple in the astral realm. If the location is not appropriate, Horus will tell you or suggest a location, but it is best to begin with a destination in mind.

Enter into a meditative state and perform the Majick Room Meditation from **Chapter Seven**. Go to the velvet curtain gateway and call upon Horus.

Horus the Younger,
Child King of Isis and Osiris.
Horus the Avenger,
Wise warrior of Egypt.
I ask for your power and protection.
Please come to my aid.

Open the curtain and look out into the starry cosmos. Feel a presence approaching you, taking the form of a beautiful hawk-headed man. The god Horus steps out from the gate and stands before you in your inner majick room.

He asks you where you wish to go. Tell him, and if this destination is correct and good for you, he agrees. If not, he will offer an alternative location.

Once you have decided upon the location, he seems to take off his hawk head, like a helmet, and put it upon your own head.

With this act of majick, you become the hawk Horus. You feel your beak. You see through hawk eyes. Your arms fold back, shifting into wings resting upon your body. Your feet become the claws of the hawk. You and Horus become one. Along with his form, you feel his wisdom, power, and sense of true sight entering your consciousness, guiding you. You see things sharply, as they really are. Nothing, including yourself, can fool you now.

You take flight through the gateway, soaring towards your destination, wherever it might be.

You arrive at your destination. Like a powerful act of remote viewing or astral travel, Horus acts as your vehicle, your chariot, to arrive at your destination and interact with whatever you perceive. Explore. Ask questions and find yourself hunting down and knowing the answers. When unsure of what to do, ask in your mind for Horus' help, and he will guide you.

When your exploration is complete, find yourself flying back towards the gateway of your majick room. Find yourself entering the gate and becoming yourself once again, returning the hawk head to the image of the god Horus. You and Horus are now two separate beings, and you give thanks to this god. He gives you any final guidance he has and then departs through the gateway. Close the curtain behind him, and when you are ready, return normally from your majick room to waking consciousness.

THE BARGE OF RA

Ra is the Sun god, the embodiment of the Sun itself. He is the head of the Egyptian pantheon and, in some stories, the creator of the world. The Egyptians had many creation stories, for they knew that these were not literal truths, but ways to look at the world. Ra is considered to be the father of the gods and the first divine pharaoh. The importance of the Sun cannot be diminished. It was particularly emphasized in ancient Egyptian religion and majick. The Sun "rules" life on this earth as it is the source of energy and potential power. Ra's power brings things into manifestation as the potential light of the Sun gives rise to plants, animals, and our entire ecosystem. Ra can help you understand those patterns. He is a source of healing and well-being. Many aspects of Egyptian life and teachings revolve around the power of the Sun giving rise to all else. The Sun and Moon were considered eyes of the gods, particularly Ra and Horus, and considered powerful protective talismans. The Eye of Ra was depicted as either the stylized right eye representing the Sun or as a solar disk flanked with two cobras, each wearing one of the crowns of Egypt.

Fig. 6: The Eye of Ra

In later myths, Isis seeks to master all majick, and Ra is the strongest source of majick. She "tricks" him out of his secret name, for anyone with the secret name of Ra has mastery of all his power. Names have power, and the Egyptians believed that to have the true name of someone or something, its *ren* or soul name, gives you its power. At this time, the elder Ra was holding onto his throne and not letting the next generation take their rightful place. Isis fashioned a cobra out of his spittle and clay. The cobra bit Ra, but since it was made from his own body, only his own majick would cure him. He didn't know the origin of the cobra, so he allowed Isis, the great magician, to "try" to cure him, with no success. She convinced him she needed his true name to have the power to cure him, and eventually he gave it, and she became an even more powerful magician, having the power of the Sun. The next generation of gods takes their role in the creation, and she passes the name onto her son, Horus, who can assume his role as pharaoh, and Ra and Horus become further associated together.

In other myths, Ra travels the sky in his solar barge, with a retinue of gods who guide and aid him. As the Sun travels east to west, so does he. When the Sun sets, the boat enters the underworld and must be defended against the forces of chaos and destruction in the form of a great serpent Apophis and his own monstrous allies of the underworld. Successful defense grants the world one more day of light as Ra is reborn at dawn.

Often appearing as a falcon or hawk-headed god, Ra can also take the form of a ram, phoenix, bull, lion, or scarab beetle. At times, he is simply depicted as an old man made from precious metals and gems. He can be called upon for health, blessings, and power, but he also calls upon us to be beacons of his light in the world.

Prepare by lighting a white or gold candle. If you have an image of the Eye of Ra, place it before the candle. Light some frankincense incense, or if you have access to traditional Egyptian kyphi incense, burn it.

Start the Egyptian Sun meditation as found in **Chapter Four**. Continue until you cross your arms over your heart in the Egyptian God position, like a mummy. Now feel the Sun overhead descend down around you, as if you are rising up to meet the Sun. Release your arms and hands and rest them in your lap. You are surrounded by the golden bright sphere of energy, and you realize you have entered the Temple of Ra. Attuned to the life force of the Egyptian Sun, you can now commune with the first of the Sun gods, Ra. You are surrounded by light.

The Temple of Ra is also the barge of the Sun, the boat that for millions of years has traversed the sky and descended into the underworld. As the brilliant light fades, you see the falcon-headed Ra. Upon his head is the great solar disc and the coiled serpent at his brow. On either side of Ra are cobras. The cobra to his right wears the white pharaonic crown of Upper Egypt, and the one to his left wears the red pharaonic crown of Lower Egypt. Around him, in his court, are many of the gods of Egypt, his allies and defenders entering the underworld, including Set. Here enemies upon Earth are no longer enemies. All must work together for the continuation of the world.

Will you help Ra maintain the light upon the world? Will you be a force for life upon the world? Will you protect the world against forces of harm and abuse? If you agree, Ra will help you. He places the charm of the Eye of Ra upon each of your energy centers blessed by the Egyptian Sun. One form of the Eye of Ra is the right eye amulet, while the left is the Eye of Horus. The eye is protective and destructive, embodying the power of many different goddesses, including the snake goddess Wadjet, as well as the lion-headed Sekhmet, cow goddess Hathor, and mother goddess Mut. The eye defends Ra and defends the world.

Ra places the mark of his eye upon your crown at the top of your head and into your pineal gland. You will use your psychic gifts for the betterment and protection of the world.

Ra places his mark upon your throat and into your thyroid gland. You will speak words of blessing and protection.

Ra draws the eye upon your heart and into your thymus gland.

Ra marks your solar plexus, blessing each of your adrenal glands.

Finally, Ra marks your right and left palms with his eye, to do the good work in the world.

Perhaps Ra will whisper a secret name, a word of power, to help you in your journey, not unlike Isis receiving his secret name.

Ra thanks you for your coming work as a protector and defender of life and light in the world, and he returns you to the world as you fill with light and become one with the sphere of the Sun again. The Sun returns you to where you began, back to your body. Give yourself Total Health Clearance and return your awareness back to the waking world.

THE HOME OF HATHOR

Hathor is one of the most benevolent, loved, and popular goddesses of Egypt, and people are still deeply drawn to her today. She is a goddess of joy and happiness, children, love, motherhood, fertility, music, dance, and celebration. She is the goddess of all good things. Hathor assists in childbirth, but also warmly welcomes the newly dead into the next life by giving them refreshments of food and drink.

Hathor's animal image is usually the cow (cow horn iconography would later be associated with the beloved goddess Isis). Cows are traditionally a goddess symbol of the mother goddess, of giving and unconditional love. In various myths, she is the wife to either Ra or Horus.

In some tales, her more bloodthirsty alter ego is the avenging lion goddess Sekhmet. When Ra wanted to punish humanity for its wickedness, he sent her forth as Sekhmet, and she grew bloodthirsty in her punishment of humanity, relishing in destruction. Soon the gods realized she would go too far and destroy everyone. They schemed to stop her rampage by gathering many jars of beer, lacing them with a powerful herb such as mandrake, coloring the liquid red, and telling her it was blood. She happily drank what she thought was blood and was pacified, returning to the form of benevolent Hathor.

I seek out Hathor as a goddess of comfort. She is always there in her comfortable dwelling, offering shelter and sustenance. In my visions of Hathor, she is a goddess of hearth and home. She listens deeply and gives food and drink.

> Light a turquoise blue or white candle for Hathor. Place a glass of milk (for her cow associations) or simply clear water next to it. Enter into a meditative state. Use the Majick Room Meditation from **Chapter Seven** to enter your own inner sacred space. Go to the velvet curtain gateway and call upon the goddess Hathor. Through the gate, you see into her home. There is the goddess Hathor, wearing a Sun disk crown with cow horns, yet otherwise looking very relaxed and informal. Around her neck is a turquoise necklace. There is no pretense or formality. She invites you into her home. You step through the gate and enter the world of Hathor.
>
> Her home has a fireplace going with a cooking pot hanging inside. She is making all sorts of marvelous foods and drinks. It smells wonderful, like all of your favorite foods. She invites you to sit down, as if she were a mother inviting you to sit at her kitchen table while she works.
>
> In the background you hear soft and relaxing music. Hathor speaks to you and immediately puts you at ease. She asks about you, about your day and your life. You speak to her as if she were an old friend, for in many ways, she is.

Tell her about your life. Tell her about your troubles. Ask her for advice. She will approach you with warmth and compassion, teaching you to see the blessing in all things.

She serves you some food and drink. It is your favorite food in the world. How did she know? With each bite, you feel yourself empowered and healed. You feel joy and love in your heart. You welcome the blessings of life.

When you are done visiting with Hathor, she'll gently nudge you out, telling you she has many others to help as well. She brings you back to the gateway of your majick room and tells you that you can return anytime you need her help and support.

Pass back into your majick room and close the curtain behind yourself. Give yourself Total Health Clearance and return to waking consciousness. Snuff the candle and reuse it when you want to return to Hathor. Offer the milk at the roots of the nearest tree as an offering of thanks to the great goddess Hathor.

THE MEDITATION OF SEKHMET

Sekhmet bears the face of a beautiful lioness with golden fur and amber eyes. She is graceful and feminine, yet wields the power of the lion. Sometimes depicted with the Sun Disc on her head, signifying her partnership with Hathor, she carries an ankh of life in one hand and in the other, a scepter made from papyrus signifying Sudan or lower Egypt, where lions are plentiful. She is said to be the goddess of healers. Known as both the creator and destroyer, Sekhmet is also the patron of physicians, and her priests were all doctors and surgeons. Above all Sekhmet is the protector of Ma'at, which means balance or justice. She is known as the one who loves Ma'at.

Created by Penny Cabot, this meditation to connect to the lion goddess of Egypt should be done at midday when the Sun is at its highest point. To perform it, you will also need to put your bare feet into a tray of sand. It is best to purchase new, clean sand and to use something flat like a baking pan or an old sheet. If you would like to enhance this Egyptian experience further, you may also fill a bowl halfway with sand and place the bowl on your lap to run your finger through as you work through this beautiful Sun goddess meditation. A citrine stone can be added to the bowl of sand.

At midday, sit comfortably in a chair with your feet in the sand. Move your feet gently as you begin to relax your mind and body. Feel the stress of the day melt away, starting from the top of your head and moving down your body, relaxing your eyelids, your neck, and your shoulders. Feel the sand slipping through your toes and fingers as you feel the Sun's rays on your face. Relax in this space as long as you need, connecting to the deserts of Egypt, connecting to the goddess. When you are ready, call her name three times: *Sekhmet, Sekhmet, Sekhmet.* Count down into alpha.

Envision the goddess before you; speak your name and introduce yourself. See the sensual slender feminine body and her powerful lion face with soft amber eyes. Ask her of her knowledge. Ask her, "What do I practice?" She will reveal to you what is most needed in your life, whether it is healing, justice, or pestilence.

If she reveals pestilence, this will indicate that there are aspects of yourself you need to shed in order to move forward in your life. Are there negative influences of others affecting your life? Are there old ways that need to be released? Her words now begin to cleanse this incorrect energy from your being and your aura. Speak,

"I cleanse my energy of all incorrect energies and forces that may reside to do harm."

For health, ask Sekhmet to send her priests of medicine for healing.

For justice, speak the word *"Ma'at"* three times.

Reside in this space with the goddess as long as you need and thank her for her time. As you feel the sand again between your fingers and toes, visualize the Sun's rays of yellow and gold being absorbed into your body. Speak,

"I bring back with me the ability of creation and the ability of pestilence. Creation for all aspects in my life I wish to grow for the correctness of all. Pestilence to rid my life of all negative or positive people, energies, and forces that may come to do harm. I ask this for the good of all and harm to none."

Relax and absorb these words. Give yourself Total Health Clearance. When you are ready, you may now count up from alpha.

You can save your sand if you like, keeping it for future use. Leave a citrine stone in the Sun with some of the sand as an offering to the goddess Sekhmet.

THE TEMPLE OF CATS

Bast is the ancient Egyptian goddess of cats. Being a deity of primal forces, protection, and warfare, she most likely originated in the ancient and fiery lion goddesses, such as Sekhmet. Over time, she transformed into the domestic cat goddess familiar to us today. While originally more solar, the Greeks associated her with Artemis, lending her Moon goddess associations over time.

Witches particularly love her as a protector of cats, since so many of our familiars are cats. I have always had a black cat, but not always by choice. Even when people didn't know I was a Witch, they would give me black cats. They have kindled my majickal understanding of all cats, big and small, and helped me see the spiritual connections between our familiars and the great cats of the jungle. Other deities, such as Freya, have cat associations. Cat goddesses are powerful and wise keepers of mystery.

Since I have had so many cats, Bast has naturally been a part of my life. I see her either as a large black cat or as she is traditionally depicted in her statues, as half-cat and half-human. She is the goddess to go to when you need advice, when you need to see your situation clearly. Go to her when you need help with a difficult problem. She will cut to the heart of it.

> To begin, light a white or black candle to Bast. If you have a statue or image of her, place it next to the candle. A small bowl of milk as an offering is appropriate.

> Enter into an alpha state. Think about the bowl of white milk and how it is not unlike the full white Moon. Picture the Moon on the screen of your mind, and the milky white Moon becomes a portal. You enter the Moon gate and find yourself walking a sandy path in the desert. In the distance is the Temple to Bast, made from a light brown stone, glistening in the moonlight against the darkness of the night sky. You see the Moon reflecting off the water surrounding the temple and approach it.

> As you enter, you see many statues of cats, lions, and cat goddesses. Some are made from granite, others from a black

basalt. The temple has many flesh-and-blood cats wandering around, as if the temple was built for them to come and worship, not humans. Humans honor Bast by honoring the cats, and you are greeted by a silky black one. It might allow you to pet and scratch behind its ears. As you show affection for the cat, you show devotion to Bast.

The cat leads you to the center of the temple. There upon a luxurious "throne" of pillows and cloths sits Bast, mistress of the night. She is as she is portrayed in her statues, part human and part cat. She holds the sistrum rattle in her hand and shakes it gently.

Speak with Bast. She is both cautious and bold, like a cat. She will teach you to stalk your prey, and your first prey should be true knowledge. She will ask you bold and hard questions. She will teach you about your own personal situations, but also about the cosmos and creation. How did things come about? Where did it all come from? Where is it going? Why? The answers are the same for the big questions and the little questions of life.

Bast will teach you to be cautious, to rethink things and be certain, to assess your situation and then take action and follow your instincts. She can teach you how to be invisible and how to see through the eyes of a cat, to see truly.

Bast will make it clear when your audience is over. Thank her and follow the path back out of the temple. The Moon is now setting in the west, and you follow the path where the horizon and the Moon meet, returning through the Moon portal back to your place and time. Give yourself Total Health Clearance and return yourself to waking consciousness. Make an offering of the milk to your own cat, or to stray cats outside, to honor Bast.

THE PYRAMID AND THE SPHINX

Modern mystics are still fascinated with the land of Egypt. Christian psychic Edgar Cayce, known as the Sleeping Prophet, gave many famous readings on past lives and healing in which he said that there is a mysterious Hall of Records, detailing the history of the world before the Great Flood, and that the records are found in a hidden underground chamber near the great pyramid in Giza, with its entrance near the ancient Sphinx. Controversial research has dated the pyramids and Sphinx as far older than most Egyptologists believe. Like many other psychic adventurers, I've encountered in my own visions a chamber in the sands of Giza that appears to be a Hall of Records, some sort of spiritual interface for what people call the Akashic Records, the wisdom of the Divine Mind. You too can go there and get answers about the world, its history, and the true story of humanity.

Count down into an alpha state of meditation. Envision your awareness rising up from where you sit, to come upon the rooftop of your building or home. Draw a glowing white light pentacle upon the roof to mark the place where you begin and end, a homing beacon to return to. Once the pentagram is drawn with this intention, feel yourself ascending upwards, rising high into the sky.

Take a moment to look down. See the building, the rooftop, and your glowing white light pentacle. Intend to travel towards Egypt, and much like the Crystal Door meditation, find yourself rushing towards the direction of Egypt, with the sky all around you rushing by and the images of the land and oceans beneath you blurring as you go.

Find yourself arriving in Egypt and see the Nile River beneath you. There are modern buildings and cities, but it is also the ancient sites that catch your attention. You are drawn to the area of Giza, where the three most famous pyramids are, along with the Sphinx, not too far from the Nile and near the modern city of Cairo.

You "land" from your psychic flight next to the Sphinx, the great guardian. There are said to be four teachings associated with the Sphinx and the elements, with majick and the Witch's Pyramid. The Sphinx asks us "to know, to will, to dare, and to keep silent." Gaze upon this ancient statue and feel the presence of the divine wisdom emanating from it.

You see a special, secret doorway between the front paws of the Sphinx and know you can enter. You move into a secret passageway that descends under the ancient complex, into the stone and sand. You come to a doorway that requires you go up four steps and enter onto a platform. You might feel as if you are being examined or tested. Walk across the platform and descend four steps and enter a long hallway.

This famous hallway is the entrance to the Hall of Records, and in a way, are the records themselves. On either side are Egyptian hieroglyphic drawings, stelles, in bright colors. Some say the secrets of the major arcana of the Tarot are hidden here. The pictures might even seem to move or communicate with you, appearing different for everyone. Despite being an ancient chamber, the air in the hall is sweet and fresh, not musty as you might expect.

If you have questions, ask them as you slowly walk this hall, and the images will tell a story to answer your questions. You might see pictures, hear words, or simply be filled with a direct knowing. Take as much time as you need in this hall and let the mysteries of the Earth become clear.

The hallway leads into the initiation chamber of the Great Pyramid, though it might appear different than you expect. It is a majickal room, with a chill in the air and beams of starlight descending down from its stone shafts. You see an undecorated burial chamber, a stone sarcophagus. You feel compelled to lie down in the stone coffin, remembering the tales of Osiris. Once you do, the starlight fills the chamber, surrounding you in a blueish majickal light. Let the light heal and transform you through the mysteries of ancient Egypt. Relax and allow the experience to happen.

When you are done, it is as if an invisible hand reaches to you and gently pulls you up and out of the chamber. The room is no longer filled with light. You know it is now time to leave, and you follow the path back.

Return through the great hallway. Has anything changed? Do you have more questions? Ask them as you walk back.

Pass up the four stairs to the platform and walk across it. Then go down four steps into the main tunnel leading up to the Sphinx. Walk back through the hidden doorway and into the desert again.

Take one last look around, and with your intention, rise up and into the sky. Journey back the way you came, drawing closer to the pentacle you created. Let the land and seas beneath you whisk past like a blur, until you return with the speed of thought to where you began. Below you, you see the white light pentacle glowing.

Slowly descend until you land safely upon the roof. As you do, the pentacle fades, and you descend through the roof into the dwelling, returning back to your body. Enter the room where your body sits and envision yourself returning to your corporeal form, letting your self-image become one with the body. When you feel you are "back," start to wiggle your fingers and toes. Adjust to your return. Give yourself Total Health Clearance, and then count yourself back up from alpha.

The Egyptian mysteries can be profound and life changing. Notice the difference in your self-awareness, majick, and life after working these visions with the gods and lands of ancient Egypt.

Chapter 10: Journeys in Avalon

The heart of our tradition is found in the myths and symbols of Avalon and the tales of Camelot, Arthur, and Merlin. When I was initiated as a Witch, my teacher Felicity passed onto me the light of Excalibur, sword to sword, or in my case, sword to letter opener, as I was a young girl and my mother would not let me have a true sword at that time. I was told the Witches of Kent were the keepers of the light of Excalibur, and it was our duty to bear it out into the world.

Since that time, I've sought the wisdom in the myths and majick of Avalon. Avalon is the otherworld of our people, the realm of the gods, spirits, and faeries. It is the realm ruled by the Lady of the Lake, known by many names. Excalibur was forged in Avalon and brought to our world to restore balance and harmony with the Earth. The tales of Arthur are of our ancestors, of a time when Avalon intersected with humanity and called us to do better for the world. We invoke the powers of Avalon to continue to walk that path, embodying the blessing and will of the Goddess in all that we do.

THE LAND OF CAMELOT

Camelot is the kingdom of Arthur, the realm prophesized by a young Merlin, who then did all he could to bring about the prophecy of the noble king, knowing that in time, it too would fall away. Yet Camelot became a prototype of ideals and what could be possible in our Western consciousness, not unlike older tales of Shamballa or Atlantis. The myth of Camelot embodies the concepts of chivalry, and the return to honoring the divine feminine and the land. We still tell these tales now of a time at the intersection—and the struggle—between old traditional majick and the new ways of the growing Christian church.

One of the first steps in attuning to the majick of Avalon is to explore the most human aspect of the tales, the land and people, before diving into the mysteries of the otherworld. I did this through a remote viewing session, traveling in both time and space, and I encourage you to do the same.

> Get into an alpha state using the Crystal Countdown and perform the Crystal Door meditation with the intention of opening the crystal door and traveling backwards in time and through space to the land of Camelot.
>
> Come through the door and find yourself flying over a beautiful green landscape. From above, you can see the whole layout of the land. In the center is a castle surrounded by dwellings. While impressive, it's an ancient castle that we might think of as a fort, not the more intricate and luxurious castles depicted in the medieval ages.
>
> The further you go from the center castle, the more rural the land and people become. The landscape is dotted with scattered cottages amid fields and farms. Cattle and other animals graze, and a variety of plants are being grown for food and trade.
>
> Rivers entwine and run through the landscape, their flowing, reflective blue a contrast to the green of the land. There are lakes, some quite large, as well as marshes. In the distance you know there is the sea.
>
> Take this time to explore. Rise above or zoom in and look at the lives of the people in Camelot.

It is here—where the lands meet the waters—that the world of spirits, of Avalon, intersects with the human world. Mist and fog rise off the water every day. These are the sacred mists of Avalon. Each veil of mist is a gateway into the otherworld when the time is right.

Circle back to the center of Camelot, into the castle. Observe like an invisible visitor, viewing it all. Explore the castle, from the throne room and the Round Table to the day-to-day life of the court and knights.

When you are done with your explorations, rise back up into the sky. You can see a glimmering in the light, the frame of the crystal door, and you return to it. Open the crystal door with the intention to return to your time and place and travel through the door, letting the images rush past you on either side until you find yourself returning to your body, to your own place and time. Give yourself Total Health Clearance and return to waking consciousness.

THE ARTHURIAN KNIGHT

In the tales of King Arthur and Avalon, the Knights of the Round Table play an important role. They are champions of the virtues, brave warriors seeking out the mysteries through heroic acts. In some stories, the Round Table was part of the dowry of Queen Guinevere; in others, it was majickally crafted by Merlin. Some think the Round Table is the circle of stars, with each knight like one of the twelve zodiac signs. A thirteenth seat, known as the Siege Perilous, was saved for whoever would be the Grail Knight. In versions where there are more than twelve Knights, we often have two knights per sign, one representing the day aspect and one representing the night aspect. Witches honoring the path of Avalon can call upon the knights for help and inspiration in our own quests.

Fig. 7: The Round Table

To connect with the knights, place something to represent the Round Table upon an altar or working space. It can be a carefully crafted paper circle with twelve, thirteen, or twenty-four sections, or something as simple as a round tray or plate. Upon it, place a representation of the sword. If you have a Witch's blade, an athame, place it upon the "table" on the right. Place a chalice or cup on the left. Between them place a dark blue candle. Light the candle and recite this spell before seeking the blessings of the knights.

Knight of honor, I know of your quest.
Because of you my chalice is blessed.
Grant me your strength
To follow my dreams relentlessly
So my destiny will come to be.

Gaze at the blade. Gaze at the chalice. Focus upon the flame between them and think of the Round Table, the circle that holds them all. Close your eyes and inwardly gaze upward toward the night sky. Envision space and the circle of stars all around the Earth, forming the constellations, including the zodiac signs. Observe the interaction between the light of the stars and the darkness of space.

Bring your awareness back down to Earth. Before you is a path in the darkness of night. As you walk the path, step by step, you are aware that it is a pebbled path in a garden. The white, night-blooming flowers give a rich, sweet scent. The stones move beneath your feet, making a subtle sound. Follow the path into the grove; from there, it leads to a small, rustic building.

You enter and see flickering candles and smell burning incense. This is the chapel of the knights. There you see an armored figure, helmet at his side, kneeling upon a set of raised stairs before an altar. Upon the altar is a beautiful cup. The knight is honoring the presence found in the chalice that is all chalices. He is honoring the Grail. He is honoring the Goddess. You wait and watch silently until he is done.

He steps down and greets you, as if he was aware of your presence even while praying. The Knight of the Round Table asks you what you honor. What would be on the altar for you?

The knight, like a good mentor and friend, asks you about your dreams. What do you feel is your destiny, your purpose in this life? What do you say?

The knight then offers to bring you into the Order of the Sacred Quest.

If you accept, he asks you to kneel before the altar. As you do, a cloaked figure comes from behind the altar, hidden from view until now. She is a queen or priestess, it is hard to tell, standing before you. She is the embodiment of the Grail, of the mystery of the Goddess. The knight takes out his gleaming metal sword, and for just a moment, you have a twinge of fear. She accepts the knight's sword from him and urges you to bow your head.

The lady speaks words in some foreign and ancient tongue and then places the blade on your right shoulder, raises it above your head, and then to your left shoulder. She bids you to rise and places a pentacle insignia around your neck. As soon as she does, the entire chapel fills with a gentle mist, and the lady and the knight disappear in it. The chapel begins to dissolve in the mist, and you become more aware of your body and the room. You gently open your eyes to again gaze upon the candle, the blade and chalice, and the perfect circle holding them all. You can still feel the invisible pentacle hanging upon your neck. You know you now have the blessing and strength to continue the quest for your dreams.

THE SWORD OF KING ARTHUR

Arthur is the son of Uther Pendragon and heir to the throne of Britain. His conception and birth fulfilled the prophecy of Merlin, told when Merlin was a child, envisioning the time of Arthur after Uther and the Kingdom of Camelot. In most versions of the tale, Arthur is raised apart from his father and not completely aware of his heritage, even though he came from noble family. He was raised in the arts of battle, but not quite prepared to be a priest-king in the mysteries. Arthur was flawed and entitled. His emotions ran high, and he didn't always contemplate the consequences of his actions. I think that is why Merlin has such a hard time guiding him, and perhaps Camelot would have lasted longer if he had been a wiser king.

The role of Arthur in these troubled times was like that of an Egyptian Pharaoh. To Witches of the Avalonian Mysteries, he was to be a priest-king, the sacred sovereign uniting the people with the Goddess. He is a warrior and protector of the people, like kings before him, but also a vessel for the solar force, the sacred masculine. Beyond the Sun, he is linked with the mysteries of the stars. Arthur's name is related to the word "bear" and to the constellation Ursa Minor, the Little Bear, which contains the current pole star of our age, Polaris. One line of mystical thought teaches the King of Camelot is linked with the center of the sky, around which an Avalonian or Glastonbury Zodiac turns.

Arthur is declared king through the test of the sword in the stone. While most people focus upon Excalibur as Arthur's majickal sword, Excalibur was given to him by the Lady of the Lake and was not the same as the Sword in the Stone, which according to legend, was a sword that appeared embedded in an anvil upon a stone. After Uther, during a time without a king and after much conflict, it was believed that only the true sovereign of the land could pull the sword free from the stone. Some say Merlin placed this test to prepare the world for Arthur. Many tried and many failed. It was in the famous *Le Morte d'Arthur* by Sir Thomas Malory, quoted later by T. White in his novel *The Sword in the Stone* and in Disney's film adaptation of the same, that we have the line, ""Whoso pulleth out this sword of this stone and anvil, is rightwise king born." The boy Arthur comes along and is the only one able to pull out the sword, and he is soon recognized to be king. Many tales, including the popular classic film *Excalibur,* equate the two swords, but originally, they were different. The "sword in the stone" motif is most famous for Arthur, but it appears in other forms, particularly with the knight Galahad, who goes on to be one of the Grail Knights in later legends.

Majickally there is a lot of symbolism in the Sword in the Stone. Stones are a symbol of elemental earth, and obviously a part of the Earth Mother, a form of the Great Goddess. Swords are tools of elemental air, representing truth, or fire, or light. The unsheathing of the sword from the metal and stone shows the truth of who is really the king. While earth is a feminine element, air and fire are masculine. The sword embedded in the anvil—the iron and blood of the planet Earth and a symbol of testing and tempering—shows a union between the masculine and feminine, the sky/Sun with the land. Even later, Arthur's second sword Excalibur comes from the feminine element of water, said to be forged in Avalon, or even in the majickal lake itself, by the Lady of the Lake.

This elemental symbolism points to the union of the feminine and masculine, that the king can only rule by the blessings of the Goddess of the Land, and later the Lady of the Otherworld. The sword becomes a sign of both blessing and duty, and when the work is done, the power loaned must be returned to the land and water. There is an old covenant in the Arthurian tales between the ruler of the people and the blessings of the land and the spirit. We find the same idea throughout Celtic cultures, where a ruler must be blessed by the Goddess of Sovereignty. The blessings and union are not exclusive to the king, but also include the knights seeking the Holy Grail, the cup or cauldron of the Goddess, and the mysteries between Merlin and the Lady of the Lake.

We can follow the path of the mystery and seek our own truth and form our own covenant between the divine masculine and feminine. We are all warriors and rulers, and whether we are female or male, we can follow the path of Arthur and the knights and seek our own sword in the stone.

Start with a stone, a rock, or crystal that is special to you. Place a double-edged blade—be it a sword, athame, or even letter opener—on an altar before the stone. Behind the stone place a red candle. Light the candle in honor of King Arthur and his quest for the sword. Connect to the chain of warriors of the Goddess who have come before you.

Breathe deep. Relax your body. Gaze at the stone, blade, and candle. Your intention is to receive the blessings of the Earth Goddess to gain your sword. Feel the presence of these three sacred powers—stone, blade, and light—and when you are ready, close your eyes. Enter into a meditative state.

Envision before you a clearing, and in the center of that clearing, a large stone with an anvil upon it, a sword embedded into both anvil and stone. Carved into the stone are these words: "Whoever pulls out this sword from this stone is a true sovereign born."

Enter the clearing. Stand before the stone, anvil, and sword. See the light glistening down upon the metal, reflecting and shining back upon you. Reach out and touch the stone. Feel the heartbeat of the Earth. Feel the presence of the Mother. Will she speak to you through the stone?

Soon you realize there is a crowd gathering around you. Who is in the crowd? You might see familiar faces from your life, both supporters wishing you well and antagonists wishing for other things. They all know you are here to pull the sword as King Arthur once did. Are you ready?

Grasp the hilt of the sword and reflect upon your relationship with the Earth Mother, with the divine feminine. Are you in right relationship? Are you sovereign in your life? Are you ready to be in greater partnership with the gods not just for yourself, but to make the world a better place? If yes, you can most likely pull the sword. If not yet, you will either gain the sword to help you accomplish this, as many say King Arthur himself was not yet ready, or you'll have to return and try again.

Can you hear the cheering and the ridicule of the crowd? How does it make you feel? Does it matter at all?

With all your majickal will, pull the sword.

Take time to reflect upon the result of your action and any intuition you receive about what is next.

Take the sword if you have it and make your way through the gathered crowd and out of the clearing.

Now that you have the energy of the sword, return to your bodily awareness. Give yourself Total Health Clearance and return from your alpha level.

THE HEART OF QUEEN GUINEVERE

Queen Guinevere is a mystery, even for us today. Her tale was written in an unsympathetic way, rarely revealing her character until it became popular to characterize her as a figure similar to Eve in the Biblical Garden of Eden. When the Christian elements are emphasized in the tale, Guinevere becomes the scapegoat for everyone's poor choices, Morgan becomes the villain directly causing harm, and Merlin is the son of the Devil! But we know these stories have deeper roots in the ancient Celtic past, and through our meditations and rituals, we can connect to these ancestral heroes and see what they can teach us about their stories today. Through this, modern majickal interpretations of Guinevere show her to be a priestess of the Goddess, a warrior queen, an avatar of the Goddess, or even a faery being.

In my own visions of Guinevere, she is a figure of love and the quest for love. Her marriage was arranged while she was very young, a tradition common at the time. The Round Table was given as a dowry. She did not marry for love, for she loved another. She was not a woman empowered. She was a kind and loving queen, good to everyone and beloved for it, though her motive was to find love herself through other people. She was seeking any attention and couldn't say no, spending time with her ladies-in-waiting while Arthur was off adventuring. When I meditate upon her, I see her alone in the castle, focused on healing her loneliness and finding true love.

Today, wiser in Otherworld experience, Guinevere seeks to help us understand our own quest for love.

Build a focus for Guinevere. Start with a green candle and a green or pink stone, such as a green aventurine or rose quartz. If you have rose incense, you can burn it, or you can mist rose water. All will help you attune to the power of love and the majick of Guinevere.

Repeat the Land of Camelot meditation, but rather than exploring, enter the castle and seek out the chamber of the queen.

You find her in a high tower, brushing her hair and gazing into the mirror. Guinevere seems melancholy. Yet she notices your spirit enter the chamber even though you are invisible. We don't tend to think of Guinevere as psychic, but she senses your heart and welcomes you.

She invites you to gaze into her majick mirror. You turn from an invisible spirit into your ideal self-image. How do you look?

She speaks to you of love and the quest for love. The quest of the maiden and queen is not unlike the quest of the knight and the king, seeking the holy grail. Both must find it within before they ever find it outside of themselves. The quest, the landscape, the marriage bed, the battlefield, and even the castle are all a part of our inner reality as much as our outer life. We must seek and find our source within before we can share it with others.

Guinevere picks up a jeweled necklace with a large emerald and many diamonds upon it. She places it around your neck, and the emerald stone hangs right at your heart. You feel it vibrate and hum, like a living creature. The stone vibrates in harmony with you, and soon beats like your own living heart, filling your spirit heart and spirit veins with emerald green light of true love, the love found in the land. It is the love we must seek within. Allow the love to circulate its green light within and around you, into your aura, until you become like an emerald sphere of light.

She removes the emerald necklace, but the green light remains. She urges you to return through the crystal door as you came, bringing this green light of her love back to your body. You thank Guinevere, and she tells you can return anytime you need to learn and feel more love. You rise up out of the castle and return to the crystal door. Images rush by you as you travel back to this place and time. Your awareness is reunited with your body, and you are filled with emerald green light, anchored in your heart space. Feel the love within you, becoming a part of your very being. When you are ready, give yourself Total Health Clearance and return to waking consciousness.

THE PATH OF MERLIN

Merlin is one of most important figures of the Arthurian Saga. Known as Arthur's magician and advisor, Merlin is a masterful Witch, a wise teacher, and a trickster. He's an excellent guide for us in the ways of majick, but you might get more than you bargain for when you call upon him.

There are many stories of Merlin, and none of them are completely correct because you cannot pin him down to any one thing. As a boy, he was said to have prophesized at the Tower of King Vortigern and to have had a hand in releasing the red and white dragons. Merlin is the wild man of the forest. He gives prophecy while looking at the stars. He is the wizard crafting his potions and working with the elements. He is the partner to the Lady of the Lake, the priestess of Avalon. He was the grandmaster of the Round Table and the vision keeper of Camelot, guiding Arthur and the knights.

To work with Merlin, place a blue candle before you. Use items to build a small shrine that will help you connect to him; pine, oak, fir, hazelnuts, and mushrooms are sacred to him, so any of these can be placed around the candle. A forest-scented incense or oil is helpful. His totem is the falcon, though many associate him with owls, so a feather is appropriate on the altar. Quartz crystal, such as a crystal sphere, is also appropriate, but a rough rock of white quartz found in nature is a great connection to his power. The stone Merlinite, a form of agate, is named after him and attunes us to the elemental forces of majick.

Build your Merlin altar, and then work with either of the two Merlin meditations below.

The Three Gold Rings of Merlin (Protection & Blessing)

This protection meditation uses the image of three rings. If you have three gold or golden-colored rings, you can place them with the altar, or simply draw three rings in gold ink upon paper and place it before you.

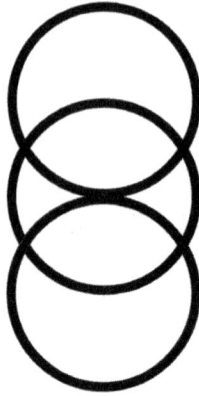

Fig. 8: Three Ring Knot

Recite this incantation before entering a trance state.

Merlin,
Place a ring around my face.
Grant me Witch's Sight to see all things right.
Place a ring around my heart
so lasting love will start.
Place a golden ring around my feet
Stepping towards my love to meet.
So mote it be.

Stare at the blue candle. Gaze into the flame. Relax your body. Clear your mind. Close your eyes and look within. In the distance, you see a pinprick of light. With each breath, it grows larger, as if moving towards you, getting closer. In the light you start to see the silhouette of someone. You realize that it is the outline of Merlin. You have called, and he has decided to come. With each moment, he grows closer until he is standing before you. You can feel the majick crackling all around him.

Introduce yourself to Merlin, though you have a feeling that he already knows all about you.

Merlin is holding a beautiful wand. With this wand, aglow with power, he begins to draw a ring of light around you. First is a ring around your face. You feel your third eye awaken with power. Your Witch Sight is active and blessed. All fears, all blocks to your true sight, dissolve away.

Merlin then takes his wand and draws a second circle, this one around your heart. Feel the energy of your heart open. Any wounds from past relationships, or from past family, all start to heal. All unnecessary guards to your heart fall away, revealing the beautiful love in your heart. Your heart pulses like a living emerald in your chest.

Lastly, Merlin takes his wand and projects a circle around your feet. You are ready to walk your path. You are ready to do the things you are here in this life to do. You are ready to meet the right people, both the ones who will help you and the ones whom you will help.

Thank Merlin for these blessings and ask if there is anything you can do to help him. Listen closely. Trust your feelings.

At the end of the work, before snuffing the candle, recite this final blessing:

Merlin,
I wear your three gold rings.
Teach good majick to me,
Power with restraint
And for the good of all.
So it shall be!

Merlin will be working with you in your meditations and dreams, and the three rings can better prepare you for the mighty Merlin working.

The Power of Mighty Merlin (Empowerment)

Enter into this meditative vision to increase your majickal power. The dragons associated with Merlin in his vision at the tower were red and white. In the Arthurian tale, many say the dragons symbolized the native British of Arthurian times (the people of Wales) and the Saxon invaders. The red dragon later became the symbol of the country of Wales.

Fig. 9: The Flag of Wales

But there is a mystical side to the dragons. They embody the energies that lie within the ley lines deep in the heart of the Earth, as well as the twin forces that are in our own bodies. The dragons flow with the power of the Sun and the Moon, fire and water, and bring majickal inspiration on our path.

Use the altar you built for the previous meditation, with the blue candle and three gold rings. Recite this call before entering a trance state.

Merlin,
Raise the Dragon's breath.
May your power protect me.
I light a blue candle to honor you
and light your way to me.
I wear your three golden rings.

Focus upon the flame of the blue candle until your eyes grow heavy and your body relaxes into a meditative state. Again, far from you, you see the pinpoint of light in the distance, but rather than feel as if Merlin is coming to you as he did previously, you must now go to him. With each beat of your heart, you grow closer to that point of light as it grows larger and larger. You sense a cool breeze from the light, and realize the light is a doorway.

Pass through the doorway. You appear on a great hillside with a tower on top and a cave opening beneath the tower. You feel the mountain breeze upon your face. The wind is filled with the subtle scent of wildflowers and the forest. You gaze up into the sky and see a falcon flying far above the tower.

In the cave entrance is Merlin, with his ancient staff, beckoning you to come inside. You follow him into the cool darkness. As soon as you enter, you feel the presence of the three gold rings about you, at your head, heart, and feet. Merlin instructs you to stand in the center of a circle in the cave. He then stamps his staff down three times upon the cave floor, and there is a rumble, like an earthquake, though you feel perfectly safe in the circle.

Beneath you, your feet feel both hot and cold. You sense an energy rising, white and red. This is the power of the two dragons. The cold white dragon rises up and enters your right foot, while the hot red dragon enters your left foot. They rise to the base of your spine and begin climbing your spine like a DNA helix, passing through the heart and making their way into the head. From your crown pours forth a fountain of stars that rise and then fall at your feet. The circle around you fills with starlight, until you are in a majickal sphere of stars.

These stars will empower, protect, and guide you on the path of the Witch. While they start to fade from your awareness, they are always with you.

When the process is done, Merlin will guide you out of the circle and out of the cave. Before you go, he might have a "mission" for you, something you must do in the world to help others. Follow the guidance of Merlin and perform the majick and service that helps bring about another age of Camelot.

Bring your awareness back to your body. Feel your fingers and toes. Return and write down any instructions Merlin gave you so that you don't forget.

AVALON AND THE LADIES OF THE LAKE

The most mysterious figure in the myths of the Arthurian romances is the Lady of the Lake. She goes through many names, and her character seems to get split time and again, creating villains and antagonists. In the earliest tales, she was Morgan, and she lived on an island of apples with her eight sisters. They ruled the marvelous land of enchantment. Later Morgan became Morgan Le Fey, showing her connection to the faery otherworld, but placing her firmly as a villain to Arthur and cast as his half-sister. Vivian becomes a popular name for the Lady of the Lake, but later tales also have Nimue, as a young lady of the lake in training, and ultimately the downfall of Merlin. None of her names seem to suit the Lady. Morgan, Viviane, Nimue—none are her! She is the otherworldly lady who fulfills a function, like a queen. Lady of the Lake is a title of her function, and while we don't fully understand that title or its function today, she is still fulfilling it in the otherworld of Avalon.

When I encounter the Lady of the Lake, I see her as distinct from any Morgan figure. Perhaps they are relatives, or even sisters. I've encountered them together on the shores of the lake. When I visit the Lady, I see a majickal teacher living a simple life on the edges of the lake. She keeps a modest yet elegant natural home, a large cottage with a roof of thatch and bark, and her world is entwined in the lake. She gets her water for drinking and bathing from the majickal lake. She waters her garden with it. She has a deep relationship with the animals around the lake. They come and go from her home freely, and without fear. The lake is her whole life. She is a faery woman who knows the secret of the sword Excalibur.

Her teachings are on majick and manifestation. She teaches through imagination. If you can imagine it, you can manifest it. She asks you to show her something clearly in your mind and heart, to make it manifest, and the lake's majick can help empower it. She is a teacher of healing and prophecy. She saw there would be a new, better king. She was waiting for him, and she kept the sword for when he was ready. She tried to empower the manifestation of Camelot, of something better, with the majick of the lake, and Excalibur was a conduit for that intention. Today we can seek her out as a teacher of majick and healing, and she will help us grow our powers of imagination and intention.

Build a focus for the Lady of the Lake. You can place a bowl of water and a candle of either silver or black out before you. Use something white, shiny, or reflective in the bowl—a quartz or moonstone sphere, a small mirror, or a white egg. Burn a lunar or water incense, such as sandalwood, jasmine flower, or anything with heather or applewood in it.

To get into an appropriate alpha state, repeat the Land of Camelot meditation. Return to the rivers and lakes. Seek out the mist. Enter the cool wet mist and find yourself passing through a veil, a portal where you are soon entering the otherworld of Avalon.

At first it doesn't look that different from Camelot, perhaps greener than what you were expecting. There is a pleasant floral or fruit-like scent throughout the air, the smell of apples and apple blossoms upon the wind. You notice that so many of the trees are apple trees, with both flower and fruit at the same time. There are also oak, hawthorn, and hazel all around.

There is a pervading mist that seems to ebb and flow, as if the land itself is inhaling and exhaling.

Flying above the land, you see the great lake. Like a magnet, it draws you towards it.

The lake is crystal clear, almost unnaturally so, and it resembles liquid glass it is so still. The mist rolls over it, but does not disturb it.

On the edge of the lake, you see her home, the magnificent cottage of the Lady of the Lake, with her bark-and-thatch roof and small garden. And you see her, there in the garden, looking right at you, as if she was waiting for you to arrive.

You land before her, and she greets you. She has been waiting for you. She is ready to teach you majick if you are ready to learn.

The Lady takes you on a tour around the lake. She walks with you along the sandy shoreline, making a circle around the great body of water. She speaks to you in soft tones and asks you questions, determining how much you know and what she can share at this time.

She points out herbs and trees upon the shoreline and explains what they are used for in majick. There are some plants here that do not grow in either the land of Camelot or the world of humanity.

She points out the stones that dwell around the lake. Some shine like jewels and crystals, and can be used in majick.

She talks to the animals as you walk. They are unafraid. The birds in the trees greet her in song, and the animals walk up to her to be petted and stroked. Each animal is a spirit, she tells you, and she invites you to play with them as she does.

Throughout it all, she speaks about the importance of imagination, of envisioning the thing you wish to create with your majick. Your imagination is like water. It flows. It runs deep. It can freeze and even at times seem to dry up, but it will always return. She asks you about your majickal goals.

The Lady speaks to you about the purpose of Excalibur and explains why she gave it to Arthur. She points to a shining speck within the lake, and you know it is Excalibur, returned to the lake again.

She speaks to you about her relationship with Merlin, and their partnership to bring about Camelot and restore the wisdom of the Goddess.

As you almost complete the circle around the lake, she shows you the water of the lake and invites you to drink from it if you are ready. These are the waters of life and light. She cups her hands and motions for you to do the same. Are you ready to drink from the majickal lake of Avalon? Things will never be the same once you do.

You complete your loop around the lake, back to her home. She bids you farewell. Thank her for all that she has taught you. She may invite you back again. But for now, she urges you through the mists, through the portal back to the world of humanity, the world of Camelot. And from Camelot, you rise back up in the sky to the crystal door. You open the crystal door with the intention to return to your proper place and time, and you travel through the gate, letting the images rush past either side of you. Return your awareness to your body, to your own place and time. Affirm you will remember the lessons of the Lady of the Lake, for they are planted deep within you now. Give yourself Total Health Clearance and return to waking consciousness.

THE PENDRAGON

Arthur's father Uther was called Pendragon, which means "dragon's head" but is best understood as "chief of the dragons," a sign of leadership and respect. In esoteric interpretations of Arthurian myth, some think Uther is associated with the constellation Draco and the pole star Thuban, the pole star before Polaris in the Little Bear of Arthur. The lifetimes of the kings show great spans of time, and ancient myth talks about the dragon kings and priests from lost lands. Perhaps the title Pendragon is a nod to those old teachings. Some consider Merlin a dragon priest or dragon prophet, as his prophecy unlocked the red and white dragons locked within the hill beneath a tower.

The dragon itself is a power force. There are dragons within the landscape. In my travels in Britain, doing circles with my sword out among the fragrant heather, dragons seemed to respond to my work. I saw dragons of the sky formed in the clouds, dragons of fire illuminated in the light of the setting Sun. In the movie *Excalibur,* the dragon is the life of the Earth itself, seen everywhere and in everything. The Red Dragon is the dragon of the Earth Mother, like the kundalini force of the planet. She is the life force of our world.

I sought out the Red Dragon for specific knowledge, and while she didn't answer my question, the quest put me in touch with this powerful force, even though it scared me at the time. Since then I've also called upon the dragon power by conjuring dragons of white light for protection and guidance when I travel both in flesh and through psychic sight. We have already connected with the inner dragon force through the Merlin empowerment of the red and white dragons. Now we can connect deeper, to the dragon of the Earth. You can connect to the Red Dragon spirit using a similar technique that I used in my quest for knowledge.

If you have a statue, photo, or image of a dragon, place it out before you. A framed picture of the red dragon on the Welsh national flag would do well. Light a red candle. If you have dragon's blood incense, burn some to invite the dragon energy to your space.

Make sure you have a specific reason for connecting with the Red Dragon. Do you need power or energy? Are you seeking a bit of ancient knowledge? Are you in need of deep healing? Don't bother the dragon for anything trivial.

Enter into a meditative state and bring all your awareness below you, to the center of the Earth. Call to the Red Dragon. Tell her what you are looking for and what you will do with her help. As you call, feel the spirit of the Red Dragon spiraling up from the center of the Earth in clockwise rings, moving up and up. You feel the heat first as she begins to rise, and you might hear the rumblings of her roar. She will rise up with fire and light. As she reaches the top of her spiral, she will turn and face you, and in that moment, she will either fill this place with purifying flames and leave you, choosing not to answer your request, or she will help you fulfill your intention.

When you are done, thank the Red Dragon for everything, even if your intention was not fulfilled. She will either fly away to another place or another practitioner, or she will spiral downward, counterclockwise, back into the heart of the Earth. Put out any incense still burning and snuff the candle. You can use it and the dragon image to connect to her again when the time is right.

With a connection to the main powers and ancestral heroes of the Arthurian myths, you can receive instructions from them to better your craft and delve deeper into the majick of Avalon.

Chapter 11:
Walking with the
Celtic Gods

The Celtic gods are at the heart of my practice and tradition. Today we draw upon the myths and practices of the various Celtic-language-based peoples, particularly the Irish, Welsh, and Scottish, to seek out their pre-Christian practices as well as surviving lore about Gaul on the continent. Together they have created a rich brew that modern Witches can build upon in forming their Celtic spirit. The Celtic goddesses and gods have been ever-present in my life, and I continue to talk with them, call upon them, and honor them in my rituals.

It is my hope that through these meditations, you can build a relationship with these powerful beings or deepen any existing relationship. You might come to find that one or more chooses you, and when they actively choose to work with you, when your soul is in alignment with their power and purpose, many doors will open in your life, and your Witch's path will shift and deepen.

THREE SPIRALS OF THE GODDESSES

This is both a meditation and a spell to evoke the blessings of the Goddess, light and dark. The two goddesses I call upon for balance are Bridget, the goddess of healing and poetry and smithcraft, and Macha, a goddess of justice and battle. Both come from the Irish pantheon, and while not traditionally associated with each other, each are triple goddesses in their own rights. Bridget manifests with her two "sisters" and are all celebrated at Imbolc in February, while Macha is a part of the triple Morrigan, with either the goddesses Anu and Badb, or Badb and Nemain, depending on the source.

Get a piece of clear parchment paper and a black pen or marker. Draw this triple spiral upon the parchment paper in black ink. You can elaborate on the basic design however you'd like, as long as you have three spirals.

Fig. 10: Triple Spiral

For the first spiral, draw it and say:

Goddess Bridget, bring to me
All the good things that can be.

Pause a moment and feel the presence of the Irish goddess Bridget, also known as Brid. Since she is the goddess of poetry, healing, and smithcraft, think of her as a goddess of creative growth.

Draw the second spiral and say:

Love that winds and comforts me
Bring a lover that loves me.

Feel the presence of love like a thread, turning and winding its way to you. Feel that thread connecting you to a lover, a friend, someone correct and good for you.

Then draw the third spiral and say:

Macha, goddess of Justice
Find those who wish me ill.
Quiet their power.
Keep them still.

Feel the presence of the crow goddess Macha. She is a goddess of justice and balance between the spirits of the land and the spirit of the people. She is called when there is injustice, abuse, or disruptions of the natural order. Feel her quieting those who would unjustly cause you harm.

Focus on the triple spiral you created. Use it as a mandala, or what is known in the East as a *yantra,* a meditative image to connect with deeper spiritual powers. Gaze at it until your vision becomes blurry, and then close your eyes. In your mind's eye, envision the two goddesses before you, tall and powerful. One is bright and red-haired, bringing blessings to you. This is Bridget. The other is dark and raven-haired, removing harm. This is Macha. Threads wind between them, as they weave for you. Bridget's threads are bringing blessings towards you, while Macha's threads move harm away and quell those who would make harm. Gaze at the goddesses working their majick for you. They may stay silent, or they may speak with you as they work.

They might tell you what you can do to help them bring blessings and remove harm.

When they are done, they will begin to fade away, and you'll lose focus of them. Gently open your eyes and return your gaze to the triple spiral.

Give yourself Total Health Clearance and ground yourself back in this world. Either place the spiral somewhere secret in your home, to keep their presence strong with you, or burn it and scatter the cooled ashes on your land.

THE SUN GOD LUGH

Lugh is the Irish Celtic god of many skills. He is knowledgeable in all the arts, sciences, trades and majick. In his legend, he knocked upon the door of Tara, the home of the gods. To gain entry, he boasted of his many skills. While all the gods were skilled, none had learned all the knowledge that Lugh had, so he was given entry and went on to be a great leader and hero of the Tuatha De Dannan. He can help those who work with him spiritually to gain new skills and increase the gifts they already have.

To meditate upon the god Lugh (pronounced Lou), a god of light and lightning who is associated today with the Sun and golden harvest, light a yellow or gold candle. You can anoint the candle with pine or amber essential oil. If you have a gold pentacle, or other piece of majickal jewelry cast in gold, wear it to attune to the Sun's powers. Face the east if possible, gaze at the candle, and recite this spell:

Mighty Lugh,
God of the Sun,
Bring forth treasures of gold

like the light that shines upon us.
Grant to me your knowledge and just power,
For the good of all.
So mote it be.

Close your eyes and envision the horizon at dawn. The Sun is just coming up, shining rays of light through the darkness. The morning air is crisp and cool, filled with new possibilities. With each breath, with each moment, the Sun rises just a little further, and the sky is filled with a bright golden light. As you stare at the Sun, the darkened silhouette of a figure emerges from the horizon. With each step, he moves forward towards you. The black outline against the Sun's light is tall, regal, that of a warrior and king. He carries a spear with him as he walks.

The light begins to clear, and you start to see the features of this figure, and you know he is the god Lugh, answering your call. He comes closer and closer to you. You see his kind eyes as he gazes upon you. He is clad as a warrior, and his warmth combined with the warmth of the Sun brings a heat to you, balancing out the cool morning air. Step by step he comes closer until he is before you. He greets you, and you welcome him.

Lugh is here to help you find your treasure, within your life and within yourself. His golden aura radiates light, filling you with light and warmth. Your own aura fills with the golden light. Lugh asks you to think about the prosperity you need. What do you need for your treasure in the world? Do you need success at work? Do you need a new vocation? Do you need greater prosperity to meet your goals? If you are willing to apply your talents, he is willing to help you. Make your wish for prosperity and success as Lugh blesses you with his golden light.

When your aura is filled with golden light, he reaches towards you. He blesses your forehead with his hands, awaking your inner knowledge, the true treasure. He catalyzes your own inner talents to come forward and guide you. What comes to mind as your true skills that need to be explored?

He then touches your hands, blessing them with just power, the power to use your skills and prosperity for not only your good, but for the good of all. When you use your skills wisely, you help both yourself and the world. He fills your hands with power, the power to succeed in your goals.

Thank the mighty Lugh for these blessings and treasures. He says farewell to you and continues his path past you, walking from the east to the west, just as the Sun follows its daily cycle.

Return your awareness to the room and gaze at the yellow or gold candle. Give yourself Total Health Clearance and ground yourself back in this world. Let the candle burn if you can, to continue the blessing of Lugh, or snuff it out to relight again when you want to commune with him. Likewise, wear your gold jewelry to remind yourself of the treasures and blessings of Lugh. Go out into the world and seek to use these skills and powers justly. Set your goals and work towards them, knowing Lugh supports you on your path.

THE AWEN OF TALIESIN THE BARD

The tale of Taliesin is a tale of initiation in the arts of majick and poetry. He is considered the son of the goddess Cerridwen and is the primal poet and bard of the Druidic arts. Taliesin becomes the ideal and template to which all other magicians of words and poetry aspire.

One of my most profound and inspired majickal experiences occurred with Taliesin. I used a majick horn that I had crafted and filled with the finest resins and oils to help me enter into a deep trance, and then I called upon Taliesin to sing me one of his songs. He sang to me the most beautiful love songs. I was so mesmerized that a part of me feared I would never get back from the journey, and another part worried I would not remember the song. I was only able to retain a fragment of his song, and I now use it to evoke his blessing and power in my life. It was his gift to me, and a gift I share with you. If you want to connect deeply with Taliesin, I suggest building a similar horn of power.

Obtain a hollowed bull horn. Many are fashioned into drinking horns and are available through various crafting sources. Place three quartz stones at the bottom of the horn, each stone cleansed and charged. The first stone is for deep trance, the second for clear communication, and the third for total memory of your experiences. Then fill the horn with your favorite aromatic majickal resins, woods, flowers, and herbs. Use anything you feel will enhance your trance majick. Then add corresponding and complementary oils, letting them seep into the herbs and horn. I used a mixture of frankincense, myrrh, copal, dragon's blood, benzoin, and storax. Add dried flowers and leaves of lavender, heather, jasmine, mugwort, wormwood, rosemary, and chamomile. Cover the opening for at least a month.

When you are ready to commune with Taliesin, prepare a bed where you will go into deep trance and be undisturbed. On a piece of parchment paper, write the name TALIESIN with the symbol of *Awen*, or inspiration, a sign associated with the bards and druids. It is three black dots, for three drops of Cerridwen's brew, with three lines of light, surrounded by three circles. Place it beneath your pillow.

Fig. 11: Awen

Recite the poem Taliesin gave me:

I am the soft breeze that moves your golden hair.
I am the cool wind that brings color to your face.
I am the spindle that weaves the clothes you wear.
I am the fingers that sew the trim of lace,
that crown your beauty,
that warm your heart.
I am the songbird that sings your love,
that sounds your beauty,
and beats your heart.
I am the moonlight that showers your sleep,
that deepens your beauty,
that rests your heart.
I am the starlight that illumines your dreams.
Love is all that it seems.

Lie down and place the horn upon your chest with the opening towards your face. Close your eyes and breathe in the aroma of the horn, letting the scent take you deep into a meditative state. Use the Crystal Countdown, and call to Taliesin in your mind.

Upon the screen of your mind, see a forest line and a meadow of flowers and grasses before it. The Sun is setting, and from the edge of the forest comes a figure. He is playing an instrument of some sort, and singing or speaking poetry that is beautiful and haunting. The figure is in the distance, and you can't quite make him out, but with each step closer to you, he becomes clearer and more beautiful to you.

The setting Sun's rays strike upon his brow, and it is as if he lights up from within with a dazzling spiritual light. He begins to shine, and his light radiates outward, as if a star were shining through from his skull. The light, the song, the music, all entrance you. They are healing and changing you. The blessings of *awen,* of inspiration, are flowing into you. Allow inspiration to trigger changes within your soul.

When you are done, he simply waves farewell and makes his way back into the forest. His light recedes into the woods. Affirm you will remember all that he said and sang. Return from our alpha state. Give yourself Total Health Clearance and gently rise. Cover the horn again until its next use and take this time to journal on all the messages you have received.

THE CAULDRON OF CERRIDWEN

Cerridwen is the "mother" of Taliesin, for she is the mother of his initiatory rebirth. Cerridwen is the mother of two children, diametrically opposed. Her daughter Creirwy is beautiful and full of light. Everyone loves her. Her son Morfran is ugly and described as "utter darkness" or Afagddu. People fear him. Cerridwen attempts to help her son, but when none of her transformative majick works, she desires to grant him wisdom, eloquence, and majick, deciding that if people wouldn't love him for his looks, they would admire and respect his skills. To help him earn a place in the world, she brews *awen,* inspiration, in her majick cauldron. She conscribes the work of two servant/slaves: a blind old man forced to stoke the fire and a young boy made to stir the cauldron. Near the end of the brew's creation, the boy, Gwion Bach, splatters three drops upon his thumb, and naturally wanting to cool the pain of the burning liquid, sticks his thumb in his mouth, consuming the drops and gaining all the power of the potion. With his new wisdom, he realizes that Cerridwen will be angry and seek to destroy him for ruining her plans for Morfran, and he tries to escape. This leads to a chase, a series of animal hunts where Gwion and Cerridwen take on different animal shapes. Gwion eventually turns into a grain and Cerridwen into a black hen, and she eats him, becoming pregnant and giving birth to the child who would later become Taliesin, the greatest of bards, all due to her potion of *awen.*

When I think of Cerridwen, I think of all her fury and anger. She put so much effort and majick into that potion. Cerridwen trudged up hills and into meadows, through deep woods and swamps, to get her ingredients. Not only did she have to find the right plants to put into her potion, she had to also make sure the time and place were proper, that the energy was exact. Prior to even embarking upon this quest, she made a deep study of majick, seeking the knowledge of nature. Without it, she would never have been able to find those specific ingredients and know when and how to mix them. She found things under rocks, growing upon trees, near far-off lakes beyond her home. She had to travel the world, to other kingdoms and countries. In truth, she was gathering all the wisdom expressed in nature, for that was the only way the potion could distill all knowledge and inspiration.

Her intention to help her son was pure. No mother wants her child to suffer. Every mother wants the best for her children. So when that intention is spoiled by the unexpected, of course rage rose within her. Like many parents, she was infuriated at herself for her failure, and she took her anger out on Gwion Bach.

At the end of everything, I think she understood that her son was not to be the great bard. It needed to be Taliesin, and Taliesin could only come from Gwion Bach. He was meant for it all along, even if she hadn't known that at the time. Despite all our plans, the unexpected accident can lead to what is necessary for the good of all. Sometimes we—and sometimes even the gods—serve in ways we don't consciously understand or expect. By the end, as a goddess of transformation, Cerridwen became cognizant of this greater understanding and transformed her anger to reverence, setting her new "son" upon his path.

As the goddess of the cauldron, the goddess of transformation and distillation, she can teach us how to transform ourselves. We, too, often need to transform our anger and rage. We, too, need to recognize when we are serving a greater good, even when it doesn't work out in the way we expected or envisioned or when it might cause us personal failure while ensuring success in the greater community.

In addition to representing deeper spiritual purpose and transformation, Cerridwen is also a goddess of Witchcraft, especially potion crafting and herbal knowledge. We can visit with her and learn the secrets of deepening our majick skills, taking our turn stirring her cauldron.

To attune to Cerridwen for this meditation, create an altar by placing a black cloth upon a table. Place a cauldron filled with water and a sprinkling of your favorite herbs on the table. Add three black taper candles. Light the candles and recite this incantation to the goddess of transformation.

Three drops of wisdom
Three drops of inspiration

Three drops of awen
Cerridwen grant me the majick
Of the greyhound to the black hen
Teach me to change
Teach me to transform
Teach me all the ways to be reborn.

Gaze at the candles. Think about how fire transforms everything. It changes whatever it burns to heat and light, forms of energy, and to ash. That light goes forth into the universe and might later become a part of something else.

When you feel ready, close your eyes. Enter into an alpha state. On the screen of your mind, picture looking deep into a cauldron, with the water swirling around like a whirlpool. As you gaze into the spinning water, you are mesmerized. As you gaze, you are drawn in. The cauldron water acts like a portal, like a crystal door, and you find yourself swirling down a tunnel of water, like a drain, floating and never in any danger of drowning or getting hurt.

You find yourself washing up on the shores of an island, as if you were a castaway from a shipwreck. You pick yourself up, dust yourself off, and look around. The island is lush and green, but eerily quiet, as if there are no animals to make any sounds or movement.

As you explore, you see gray wood smoke in the distance, and you make your way towards the rising smoke. You soon see a hut, a type of cottage in the distance, and go towards it, knowing this is the hut of Cerridwen.

Approach with respect. Knock on the outer edges of the doorway. If she wishes to see you, she will bid you come inside where it is dark, but illuminated by flame. She welcomes you, and you see that she is stirring a cauldron. Herbs hang from the beams of the hut, drying to be used in her potions. The aroma is thick with a green quality. The flicking flames illuminate different sections of the hut. It's hard to take it all in at once.

Cerridwen greets you and tells you to sit down beside her and the cauldron. She asks what you are seeking. Take this time to talk with Cerridwen, to ask for advice, help, or specific teachings. She can sometimes be harsh, and don't be surprised if she occasionally hits you over the head with her spoon.

When you are done, thank her for everything. She may give you a sip from her cauldron spoon, but she might not. Be sure to ask her what the potion is before you drink it, though it can be impolite to turn down a goddess. She knows what you need more than you do.

Follow the path that brought you there back through the island's greenery, back to the shore where you began. Enter the water of her majickal lake, and as you dive under, find yourself being pulled up, up, up through the cauldron and back to your place in the room, in your body. Give yourself Total Health Clearance and return from your alpha state, making sure you write down and follow any advice that Cerridwen has given you.

THE VISION OF BRANWEN: HOLD YOUR BROTHERS CLOSE

In this meditation we look at the three aspects of self as represented by the brothers of the goddess Branwen: Manawydan, Bran, and the paired twins Nisien and Efnysien, who function as one. We recognize Manawydan, who rules the physical aspect of us, as the one who takes action, who rules accountability, self-recognition, and blame. We recognize Bran as the physical component, as the giant and king. And we recognize Efnysien and Nisien as the mental-spiritual component, with Efnysien as the "bad" brother who broke the cauldron that contains our spiritual and mental powers, abilities that either help us rise or that rule us, and Nisien as the balance of those energies that allows us to make good decisions. We will also connect with Branwen, who will represent you as the maiden, the mother, and the sister to her brothers, which are also all aspects of you. Penny's deep connection to this goddess has given her insight about the relationship with Branwen's brothers that she shares here with us.

Before we count into alpha, we will become familiar with Branwen. As the princess-queen of her home, she marries the King of Ireland and travels to her new home. She cooks in the kitchen with modesty and cares for family. When Branwen feels disrespected by her new husband and her current situation, she trains a bird, a starling, to send a message to her brothers to come to her aid. Like Branwen and her brothers, and like our best version of self, we try to keep a mental balance to maintain ourselves in our current journey of life, and in doing so, we recognize the mental, material, and physical aspects of ourselves all working together. You will experience each brother's actions as an aspect of yourself and correct the behavior and thinking of that brother within you so that he may function as a true extension of self.

I suggest finding a comfortable chair and softly playing some soothing instrumental Celtic music as background. Count down into alpha, relaxing your mind, breathing in through your nose and out through your mouth, exhaling all the stress of the day. Relax your shoulders. Feel the tension leave your body. Take a deep breath and exhale slowly, letting go of words, thoughts, and feelings. Your hands are relaxed, and now all the daily events have left your body. Listen to the music and call her name three times: *"Branwen, Branwen, Branwen."*

Three figures stand before you, one aspect in front of you, one aspect to the left, and one aspect to the right. Look to the brother on the left. His name is Manawydan, and he rules your material aspect. View him as you would view yourself. Inspect him closely. Does he have a beard? How is he dressed? Does he carry a pocket full of coins as a boast or as preparation for necessity? Does he wear rings of gold or boots of practicality? View this brother as this aspect of yourself. In alpha state, you may now speak with this brother. You may adjust his clothing and modify this aspect to the best and most correct version of yourself. Thank him for his time and move on to the next brother.

Look directly in front of you and see Nisien and Efnysien, the spirit-mind brothers embodying choice. They rule your mental state, making good and bad decisions, creating and destroying. Examine their clothing and facial features. Look at their body language. How do they stand? Is it with confidence? Do they fidget nervously, looking all about? Do they look directly into your eyes with kindness and confidence? Now view these brothers as another aspect of yourself. Edit the body language that does not suit you. Envision Nisien and Efnysien as the best version of yourself, tall and proud, looking directly into your eyes with kindness and confidence. Smile back and thank them for their time.

Now look to your right and view the brother Bran, who rules the physical. Look at his physical stature. Is he thin and frail, or strong and athletic? Does he wear sandals for being agile or sturdy boots for lifting heavy loads? Are his hands soft, or are they calloused from a hard day's work? Look into his eyes. Are they stern and strong, or tired and weary? Now view Bran and correct this view to the best version of yourself with strong leathered hands and broad shoulders, with a great, kind chest able to hold the pride of accomplishments realized and tasks achieved. Envision him as the best and most correct version of you. Thank him for his time.

Now envision all the brothers standing side by side, strong, kind, and well-dressed. Envision all of them stepping towards you. As you breathe in, inhale all the energy of all the brothers, breathing them deep into your lungs. You are Branwen the sister. You breathe in the love for your brothers. You feel the strength from the physical, the kindness from the mental, and the comfort from the material. Hold them deep within you like a sister hugging her brothers. You have become one.

Stay in this space for as long as you need. When you are ready, give yourself Total Health Clearance and count up from alpha level.

You may leave an offering for Branwen and her brothers by placing a coin, a rock, and a piece of cloth to signify Branwen in a small black cauldron. Place a feather to represent communication.
You may revisit this meditation any time you need to do so, and you can always readjust each brother. The adjustment will flow with your daily life and the changes you may need along your path.

MOTHER MODRON HOME BLESSINGS

Modron is the Mother Goddess of the Welsh gods. Mother of the young son Mabon, she is the Great Goddess, similar in many ways to Danu of the Irish gods. While she can be loving and caring like our image of the ideal mother, she is also primal and fierce. In many ways she is beyond anything personal, a manifestation of the source of all life. As such, she is the source of blessing and stability when called upon in that aspect.

In this vision, work with Mother Modron and bring the blessing from the source of life back to your home and family.

Prepare an altar for Modron. Gather some dirt, soil, and stones from your home. If you live in an apartment building, gather it from the nearest source, whatever is around you. Place a black candle in the center of it, but do not light the candle. Before beginning, say the words:

Mother Modron,
I seek your blessing.
May I find my way to you.

If there is a small stone on the altar, place that stone in your left hand. Roll it in your hand. Feel the texture. Connect to the Mother through the stone. Immerse yourself in the feeling of the stone as you close your eyes. Breathe deep and relax your body from the top of your head to the tips of your toes, all the while rolling the stone in your left hand.

Feel the power of gravity, the pull of the Earth drawing you deeper, connecting you to the planet as it turns in the world of stars. With each breath, feel as if you are sinking down into the land. You have no fear. You can breathe normally. You are becoming one with the land, feeling the gentle pulse of the earth beneath the homes and buildings. You can feel the veins of minerals, and the stones heave within the body of the Earth, as if the land itself is breathing.

You continue to go deeper, and as you do, you find yourself entering a vast cavern, filled with stalactites and stalagmites. You hear the dripping of ancient water from these pointed formations, dripping into cool pools, continuing this process of growth within the land. There is just enough light to see the silhouettes of these mineral formations. You see flashes of crystals and gems embedded in the walls, floor, and ceiling of the cavern. A slight chill comes over you, and you sense the deep presence of the sacred.

There in the depths, in the darkness, is the shadowed presence of Modron, the Great Mother. This cave is her home, though she is the goddess of the land everywhere. This is where you can communicate with her. Introduce yourself, though she knows who you are, as she knows everyone and everything upon the Earth. Speak with her. Speak to her about your loved ones, your family, your home. Ask for her blessings.

Feel Modron place the light of her blessing in your heart. Your heart becomes a lantern, and with this light, you can see everything in the cavern much more clearly, including Modron. You gaze deeply into her eyes. You realize that with this light, you'll see everything in the world above more clearly.

She bids you rise, and you find the weight of gravity a little lighter, allowing you to rise through the cavern ceiling up to the land. You feel as if you are swimming through the land, returning through the surface and back to the place where you began.

You can still sense the light within your heart, illuminating the world around you. Gently open your eyes and gaze at the room around you. Gaze at the altar. Gaze at the stones and soil. Look at the candle.

Rise and approach the altar. Radiate the light of your heart into the soil, stones, and candle. Speak these words:

Mother Modron,
Grant to me a home of comfort, love and happiness,
A house where everyone is blessed.

Light the candle. Once the candle has completely burned, return the soil and stones to the land where they will carry the light of Modron's blessing.

THE WITCH'S EYES WITH THE MORRIGAN

One aspect of meditation often neglected is being in meditative, mindful awareness while walking through the world. This doesn't mean you are necessarily deep in alpha, but that you are looking at the world with Witch eyes and listening to the world with Witch ears. It is about being present in all things and aware, no matter the situation, of your thoughts and your emotional state. One of the goddesses that has been most helpful in merging the meditative and ritual experience with the everyday occurrences of life is the Morrigan.

While we often invoke the Morrigan in her many forms for justice, we can hear her crow "caw" in our everyday life, warning us of danger or asking us to pay attention. With that reminder, we remember to look at the world through the eyes of the Witch, to see the subtle meanings of our actions and the actions around us, including how the goddesses, gods, and ancestors speak to us through our circumstances and other people. Sometimes the "caw" is a literal crow near you. Other times the voice of someone, or even various noises, will bring to mind the sound of the crow or raven, reminding us to look with majickal sight.

THE GODDESS OF JUSTICE MACHA

Macha is the Irish goddess known for her associations with crows and horses. She is part of the fierce triplicity known as the Morrigan, along with Anu and Badb. She is a goddess of battle, majick, and prophecy, using her sorcery to aid her people, the Tuatha de Dannan, also known as the Children of Danu. She is best known, however, for her story in the city of Ulster. There, she takes a husband, Cruinniuc, under the condition that he never mention her or her true nature. During a horse-drawn chariot race, he brags that his wife could outrun the king's horses. This boast catches the attention and the ire of the king, who threatens her husband, forcing Macha to run. Even though she is pregnant with twins at the time, she runs and wins, giving birth to the twins upon the finish line. She then curses the men of Ulster to feel the pain of birth in their greatest time of need, as punishment for the way she was treated.

Today, we call upon Macha, bringing her attention to an unjust situation. We do this by sending feathers to the place or person suffering injustice to bring her attention to the situation. She herself will decide what is the best course of action, for we humans can get caught up in emotions and biases. It can be best to have a relationship with the goddess before petitioning her aid in such situations. Perform a variation of this meditation to align with Macha before asking for her help, and then perform it in its entirety to call on her for justice.

Light a black candle. Burn dragon's blood resin upon charcoal in your thurible incense burner. If you have a black feather, hold it and recite the following:

Black wings of power,
Follow the black feather I send.
Bring injustice to an end.

Upon the screen of your mind, envision a dark veil before you, like a starless night sky. Call upon Macha in your mind and heart. The veil begins to part, revealing the shape of an immense dark goddess wrapped in a cloak of crow feathers. She reveals her face to you.

Speak to Macha in your mind. Tell her the situation. Ask for her help. She may simply listen, or she may communicate more deeply with you. When your time with her is done, thank her and then watch her retreat back behind the starless night.

Return your awareness to the room. Give yourself Total Health Clearance. Gaze at the black candle and the smoke, if it is still wafting in the air around you. Let the candle burn. Send the black feather to the person or place causing the injustice and she will follow, balancing and bringing justice as necessary to the situation. If you send it by post, don't include a return address!

THE GODDESS ARIANRHOD

Arianrhod is the Welsh Goddess of the cosmos. Sometimes described as a Moon goddess, her name is usually translated to mean the Goddess of the "Silver Wheel," which is interpreted by many as the wheel of the stars, either the zodiac belt of twelve signs or the polar stars around the northern sky. Her home, Castle Arianrhod, is also the name of the constellation Corona Borealis, or Northern Crown, further associating her with the northern stars. Other experts, such as author Kristoffer Hughes, say the origin of her name lies more with a "round mound" and relates her to the sacred land.

Her most famous story is in the fourth branch of the Welsh *Mabinogi*. She is the sister to the magician gods Gwydion and Gilfaethwy, and mother to Dylan and Lleu. In this tale, her maidenhood is tested by her uncle, King Math. In peacetime, he is required to rest his feet in the lap of a virgin maiden, signifying his bond with the land. Due to the plots of his nephews Gwydion and Gilfaethwy, he loses his previous maiden, and Arianrhod is suggested as a replacement. Arianrhod fails his tests and immediately gives birth to her son Dylan and to a creature that will eventually become Lleu with the help of Gwydion. She is humiliated in the court, and eventually places three "curses" or taboos upon her son Lleu. He shall not have a name unless she names him. He shall not bear arms unless she arms him. And he shall not have a wife from any race that is upon the Earth now. Gwydion, as guide and teacher, helps him overcome these curses.

While Arianrhod is often interpreted as an "evil" Witch figure cursing the hero, initiates of the mysteries see deeper themes of testing and trials from the Star Goddess, not unlike the tales of Cerridwen and Taliesin, though from a different mystery. Witches seek out Arianrhod as the goddess of initiation, to guide us on the path of majick. Cabot Witches wear a ring marked with stars as a sign of initiation.

> Build an altar for Arianrhod using a silver ring and five white candles in a circle around the ring. If you do not have and cannot obtain a silver ring with stars upon it, make one of paper, marking a ring of stars in silver paint. Light the candles moving counterclockwise, the direction the northern stars turn when we look at the pole star. Burn myrrh and mugwort upon charcoal in your thurible incense burner. Speak these words:

Arianrhod,
Goddess of Initiation,
I wear your ring of stars.
I dedicate my path to the study of Witchcraft.
So mote it be.

Place the ring, metal or paper, upon your finger. Close your eyes. Look down in your inner vision, as if you are looking down into the deep center of the Earth. Then with your physical eyes still closed, look up and gaze into the darkness of space, but unlike the deep Earth, you can see the sparkling of stars. The stars seem to descend like glittering dust, all around you. The stardust takes the form of a spiraling staircase, moving to the left. Despite the stairs seemingly being made of "nothing," you take a step, and then another. Soon you are spiraling upward into the night sky, upward into the stars.

The stars themselves seem to ring out with tones, like chimes or bells, the music of the stars. The Earth grows distant beneath you. Even the Sun and planets grow distant, until eventually you are beyond our solar system and entering a new realm altogether.

Above you, you can sense a structure, a castle made from stars. The path leads to the castle, and soon you stand before it. The castle is like a perfect square, with four towers and a raised drawbridge, a moat of absolute darkness surrounding it. The castle appears to be slowly revolving in space. Below you, there is the spiraling star staircase. In your mind, you recite your call to Arianrhod again:

Arianrhod,
Goddess of Initiation,
I wear your ring of stars.
I dedicate my path to the study of Witchcraft.
So mote it be.

The drawbridge slowly lowers across the moat of flowing darkness and lets you cross. You enter a fabulous castle, rich with beautifully crafted tapestries hanging from the walls. You recognize some of the scenes, scenes from *The Mabinogi*, depicting the gods of ancient Wales. You see Lleu and Gwyidon, Dylan the sea god, King Math, Cerridwen, Taliesin, Rhiannon, Pryderi, Bran, and Branwen.

The hall leads you to the throne room, and as you enter, you see a bright silver throne gleaming in the darkness, and upon it is Arianrhod, goddess of the silver wheel. She gazes deeply into your heart and takes your measure.

Open your heart to her. Share who you are, what you've experienced, and what you seek on the path of the Witch. Ask for her blessing and guidance. Show her your ring, a sign of your quest to her.

She takes you to a large round silver mirror and asks you to look at yourself and see who you truly are. As she has taken a deep look at you, she now requires you look deeply at yourself. Gaze into the silver mirror.

When you are done, the goddess might give you a new ring, a crown of stars, or a blessing. She might also have a task for you to complete before she helps you. Listen deeply and follow the wisdom of Arianrhod.

Your audience with this goddess has come to an end, and she bids you to leave her throne chamber. She points to the long hall. As you gaze at the tapestries hanging upon the wall again, they have changed. They no longer depict the gods of Wales, but scenes from your own life. What do you see?

Cross the drawbridge over the flowing darkness and step upon the starry staircase again. Turning to the right, descend downward through the stars, through the darkness of space. Step by step, return back through the planets. Gaze at the Sun. Make your way back to Earth, back to where you began. Return your awareness to your body. Open your eyes and gaze at the candles. Snuff them, moving in a clockwise direction until they are all out. Use the ring whenever you wish to connect again with the wisdom of Arianrhod.

VISITING DAGDA, THE GOOD GOD

This meditative journey will take you to the Irish Celtic father god, the Dagda, a giant among the Tuatha De Dannan, the Children of the Goddess Danu. He is a warm and welcoming god to those of good heart, and we shall visit him in his home. Penny visits with him often and has created this meditation to share her experiences with the Dagda.

Sit comfortably in a nice cozy chair. Relax your mind and body. Feel all the tension and stress leave your limbs until your shoulders are relaxed. Breathe in through your nose and out through your mouth. Then count down into alpha. Sit quietly enjoying the solace and peace of alpha level.

Visualize yourself outside your front door. Look around you. Mark in your mind any trees and make a note of your front door. Remember any other landmarks that stand out to you.

Now rise up into the sky, floating comfortably. Feel the warm breeze. See the clouds and the tops of trees or nearby buildings. Look three hundred and sixty degrees around you. Take in the view of the building and housetops. Enjoy the warm rays of the Sun. Speak, *"Brú na Bóinne"*—or in English, *"Newgrange"*—three times.

Now feel yourself descending slowly back down. Look around you and see that the landscape has changed. As you descend, you see plush green rolling hills spotted with trees. You spot the stone walls of the ancients and notice a section of wall with a large boulder next to it. As you descend, you notice the bolder is carved with a circular scrolling pattern. As you view this stone, your feet gently touch the ground. You are now in Newgrange, Ireland, known to the ancients as *Brú na Bóinne*. Breathe in the fresh air of the rolling Irish hills. Relax in this space as long as you need, until you feel ready to call the Dagda.

When you are ready, speak this chant:

Father, chieftain, music note.
Giant, good god, hooded cloak.
Father, chieftain, music note.
Giant, good god, hooded cloak.
Father, chieftain, music note.
Giant, good god, hooded cloak.

Look at the landscape until you see a figure. Let your mind bring him forth in whatever way feels right. He may walk towards you from afar; he may appear in front of you. He is known to have favor with the Morrigan, so you might see a dark-hooded woman first or by his side.

The Dagda is a large, tall man known to the ancients as a giant, one of the first race and tribe known as the Tuatha de Dannan. While they all have a tall stature, he was taller than any other.

He is also known as the father and may appear with children playing around him. He is a hooded figure who carries a tall majick staff, known as the *lorg mor'* or *lorg anfaid,* and a cauldron held across his chest by a large leather strap over one shoulder. He carries this heavy cauldron with strength and pride, for it is forever full and plentiful.

When you see this figure before you, welcome him and speak your name. Now listen in the wind and hear the sounds of a beautiful harp playing; this is the Dagda's majick harp named Uaithne. Through the music of the harp, he brings peace, happiness, and contentment. Listen for his words. On your first introduction to the Dagda, he may not speak. He may show you symbols. This meeting is like meeting a new friend.

Thank him for his wisdom and for allowing you to visit his home and land. Stay in this space as long as you need. You may see his tribe's people, the Tuatha, tall and slender and graceful, as tall as the trees. Feel the energy of the Dagda all around you. Feel the energy of the chieftain and the ability to solve any problem. Feel the art of music throughout your body. Let the spark of creativity ignite within you. You may now bid him farewell and thank him for the visit.

Now you will ascend up into the sky, leaving the rolling hill beneath you, ascending from the boulder and stone wall until they are but dots on the landscape. Look up to the sky and breathe in the fresh air, feeling the warm Sun on your face. Speak your address three times. Now look down and envision the buildings, rooftops, and houses of your neighborhood or place where you started. See the trees and other landmarks you took mental note of when you started. You begin to see your rooftop. Now you descend, more slowly as you get closer to the ground, and you see moving cars on the streets and landmarks in front of your building. You now see your front door as your feet slowly and gently touch the ground. Walk through your front door and into the space where you are sitting. You are now comfortably back in your chair. Relax and be comfortable in this space until you are ready to give yourself Total Health Clearance and count up from alpha. You wake from this meditation freshened and vibrant, with the energy of the chieftain and the ability to work through and creatively solve any problem.

Note that when you meet gods and ancestors in the otherworld, you are building a relationship with them. Not all of the things mentioned will happen on the first visit. Like any good relationship, you revisit with that person as you build respect and trust. This is a meditation to build the framework of a working relationship, a meditation you should repeat often. It is always good after a visit with the gods and ancestors to leave an offering to show your gratitude for their time. For the Dagda, play music of the harp or violin. Set out a bowl of soup or fill a small cauldron with water. Keep a journal to make notes about your visits with him. Write down any symbols he may give you or words of majick he may share.

THE NINE CHILDREN OF DANU

Danu is a mystery. Her name gives us the title of the gods of the Irish Pantheon, the Tuatha Dé Danann, or Children of Danu, yet there is very little written about her. From academic research, we assume she is the Mother Goddess, as the gods are her children, and today we relate her to other Celtic mother goddesses, such as Don and Modron. She is associated with the land itself, and many consider Ireland her body, though according to the myths, her children "landed" in Ireland from other places. This leads to the idea that she is the Earth Mother, a Celtic counterpart to the Greek Gaea. She is often associated with water, including the Danube River, as there was once a large Celtic cultural presence near the Danube. Based on this water mythology, and that the

Tuatha came in ships from far lands, people have assumed she is an ocean or sea mother goddess. Others still think of her as a primordial ancestor, the first mother to the gods and to the people. She lived in an ancient time and land, and as an ancestor, she can guide us still.

In the Cabot Tradition, we link Danu as the embodiment of the Great Goddess, the divine feminine, and the Dagda, or Good God, as the embodiment of the divine masculine. While the Dagda has a prominent role in the myths of Ireland, with his majick club, cauldron, and harp, Danu is the invisible mystery pervading all, but unseen.

The only way of interacting on a personal level with this unseen mystery is to seek Danu in vision. Even if you know the stories, or know there are no stories recorded to be known, when you dive in personally, you get other images and teachings. The Celts certainly didn't write everything down, and the direct experience of the mysteries is why it is important to investigate and meet with the gods yourself.

When I did so, many secrets were revealed to me, and I learned how I could work with her better. Seeking her in the wilds of nature, I found a very regal woman. While I would have expected an old goddess, being the mother of all these gods, she appeared as a beautiful and fairly young woman. I knew that in many cultures, the eldest of the goddesses are depicted as maidens, but it still wasn't what I was expecting.

She is a strong woman, perhaps even a trifle dominating. She has had to be, being the queen and leader of the gods. She told me that at first, she was ignorant of her position and didn't realize her relationship to everyone. She didn't think she had a role and didn't realize how many people looked to her for leadership and decisions. She never understood being adored by others. She simply is, was, and will be. It took time for her to find the balance, seeking to right wrongs in her world.

In my meditations I've asked to see her children. In that vision, instead of taking me to a forest, she took me to a throne room in a castle. It was a traditional ancient castle with thatched roof, tall turrets, and

Page 233

multiple smaller cottages connected to it, all in a circular formation. Perhaps this was a version of Tara. She appeared on a throne before me. Nine people came towards her, women and men. She announced them as the Nine Children of Danu. Some I knew, and some I didn't. In that, there is a deeper teaching about our interconnectivity through her, which is something for you to explore in the vision below, bringing together several of my experiences with the goddess Danu.

To build a shrine to Danu for this meditation, take a vessel that can hold water—a chalice, cauldron, or crystal bowl—and place a stone or crystal that is special to you inside. Have two bottles of water. One bottle is filled with pure water that can be drunk. The other is filled with saltwater or seawater. Place nine candles of assorted colors that feel right to you around the vessel. Decorate the rest of the shrine with fallen leaves and vines.

Pour first the saltwater over the stone in the vessel to make the "ocean" aspect of Danu. Then pour the fresh water into the saltwater, like the river entering the sea. Recite this:

Danu who comes from the Land Beneath the Waves
Danu who comes to live in the forest glades
Danu Mother of the Gods.

Light the nine candles, moving clockwise, and recite this:

Danu's Nine Children
Danu's Daughters and Sons
Danu's Family of Blessed Ones

Sit down in a comfortable position, looking at the stone, water, vessel and candles. When relaxed, close your eyes. Enter into your alpha meditation state. Envision the world, as if you are looking at it from space. See the blue of the oceans. See the swirling white of the clouds. Look down and see the green and brown of the land. As you breathe in and out, looking at the world from above, think about the Goddess Danu. Feel her presence. Feel her call drawing you down.

A point on the globe appears to spark with light, drawing your attention to it. It is in one of the dark green forested sections of the world. You descend towards the earth, towards the point of light.

You move through the clouds covering the Earth, feeling the wind through your hair. You move downward still, towards the surface, and you come to the edge of an immense forest.

Enter the forest. You follow a path through the green underbrush. You notice animals scurrying through it. They all seem to be leading you in the same direction, to where your soul was called down to experience Danu.

Soon you make your way to a clearing in the heart of the forest. You see a beautiful woman, a queen of the forest, sitting by herself upon a throne made from trees. She is waiting for you. The base of the throne is the stump of an ancient tree with shoots of new growth all around, forming the arms and back of the chair, holding her naturally, as if they have grown around her.

She is dressed in beautiful but simple Celtic robes of blue, green, and brown. Leaves are interwoven through the material, as if it were made from the finest and most beautiful leaves from spring and fall. Upon her head is a crown, also woven of branches, but flecked with shining gold and silver metals and tiny jewels.

At first you might fear the branches are vines holding her prisoner, but they are interwoven with her. The forest is a part of her. If you were not drawn to her presence, she would easily be invisible in these woods, blending in and disappearing to the mortal eye. But she allows you to see her as she is.

The animals give her honor as queen of the forest, and you realize flowing in the trees and vines around her is the wisdom of the Earth, and that she is both part of, and partaking in, this wisdom. She shares this wisdom with you. Commune with her.

As you sit with her in the forest, she expands her awareness, and you expand with it. Your mind is cast far to see the edge of the ocean. She reveals she came from the ocean, as we all did. She embodies the mysteries of the ocean as well as the wisdom of the land. Beneath the ocean dwell many worlds of majick. In some ways, she understands the mysteries of the ocean world better than the world of the land.

Ask to see her children, and your mind expands further, into the realm of all the gods and mortals. She shows you, one by one, nine people. Each seems to come out of the forest behind her and gather around her. Who do you see? One by one, they speak to you, introducing themselves. They could be people from Irish myth and legend, the well-known gods of the Tuatha Dé Danann. They could be important people in your life. Some might be people you have known and loved. They could be living, dead, or perhaps not even born yet, for all are her children. Take this time to speak with the nine people she brings to you.

Let the first come forward. What do you see? Who or what stands before you? How is this person dressed? Introduce yourself and communicate together. Ask why they have come and what you must know from them.

Let the second one come forward. Use your senses. Who or what is before you, and what role do they play in your life?

Let the third child of Danu come forward. Whom do you see? Communicate with this one and the work you might have together.

Sense the fourth make their way out of the forest. Take a good look. What do you see? Who is this fourth child, and why have they come?

See the fifth Child of Danu. What do you see? Are you recognizing a theme or pattern with these children? What is their significance in your life and practice?

Feel the sixth presence arrive. What do you perceive? Who or what comes out of the forest? What do they say?

Let the seventh one make their way forward. Gaze deeply and take in the presence. Commune with this child of Danu.

Let the eighth figure step out of the forest. Who or what comes forward? Are any of these figures surprising you? Learn all you can from these beings.

Let the ninth and last child of Danu come forward. Who is this final ally in the forest? What do they want from you? What do they offer you, if anything? See the council of the nine children of Danu.

Know that you too are a child of Danu, as we all are. She is the Great Mother. What work do her children have together? How do we serve her and the greatest good of the world?

When you are done, the nine children will step back, one by one, into the forest. Affirm you will remember them and all that they said.

Danu might have a last message or word for you. Thank her, and when done, bow and say farewell. Follow your path back out of the forest. Rise up again into the heavens. Look back down upon the beautiful planet and wipe the image away from the screen of your mind. Feel your awareness return as you give yourself Total Health Clearance and return from your alpha state. Take some time to write and remember all that was shared with you, and look to the children of Danu as a spiritual team of allies, teachers, and challengers in your life.

The meditations in this chapter are from my years of working directly with the goddesses and gods of the Celtic people. I call upon them in ritual and build shrines and altars to honor them, to gain their attention and guidance. I go to them, seeking them out in their own worlds, and ask for guidance and help, and I do as they ask, helping introduce their majick and stories to others. Build our own relationships with your gods. Seek them out and build a majickal life together.

About the Author

photo by Jean Renard

Laurie Cabot is a pioneer in the modern Witchcraft movement. As a teacher, author, and activist, she was one of the first to inform the public on who and what Witches are, and what they believe and practice, through many appearances on radio and television, including the *Oprah Winfrey Show*. She has championed the rights of Witches and Pagans through establishing the Witch's League for Public Awareness, and later Project Witches Protection, educating the media on inaccurate and demeaning portrayals of Witches and educating government representatives on the religious rights of Witches.

Residing in Salem, Massachusetts, Laurie has been a publicly active Witch, running several Witchcraft shops where she offered psychic readings, as well as hosting numerous classes and public rituals, including the first ever Salem Witch's Ball. She teaches "Witchcraft As A Science" to all, emphasizing meditation and psychic development, and established her own Cabot Tradition of Witchcraft. Former Governor of Massachusetts, Michael S. Dukakis, awarded her the Patriot Award for public service and declared her the "official Witch of Salem, Massachusetts." She later established the Cabot-Kent Hermetic Temple as a federally recognized religious organization for furthering the Witchcraft community and culture. She is the author of seven books, including the classic *Power of the Witch*. For more information, visit *www.lauriecabot.com*.

www.ingramcontent.com/pod-product-compliance
Lightning Source LLC
Chambersburg PA
CBHW060018100426
42740CB00010B/1520